A CENTURY IN TWO DECADES

This project is in part supported by a grant from the National Endowment for the Arts in Washington, D.C., a federal agency.

Burning Deck is an affiliate of Anyart (5 Steeple Street, Providence), a non-profit organization.

Library of Congress Cataloging in Publication Data
Main entry under title:
A Century in two decades.
  "Bibliography of Burning Deck": p. 159
  1. American literature — 20th century.
2. English literature — 20th century.
3. Burning Deck (Firm)   I. Waldrop, Keith.
II. Waldrop, Rosmarie.
PS536.2.C4   820'.8'0054   82-4335
ISBN 0-930901-00-2   AACR2
ISBN 0-930901-01-0 (pbk.)

A Century in Two Decades

A BURNING DECK ANTHOLOGY
1961-1981

edited by Keith & Rosmarie Waldrop

BURNING DECK
Providence

contents

OOO

OOO

Twenty years along and a hundred titles out, we present this anthology as a record of where we have stood and what for. In 1961, poets were supposed to be in opposing camps, often inelegantly—and inaccurately—labeled "academics" or "beats". The two most widely noted anthologies of the time, both representing the period 1945-1960, contain not a single poet in common.

Burning Deck (the magazine) disregarded this split, printing and reviewing a spread of poets wide enough that on occasion an author would complain of being published in such unprogrammatic company. Though advertised as a "quinterly", the magazine, after only four issues, gave way to a series of pamphlets and—later—books of poetry and short fiction. Our list remains eclectic, with some emphasis on experimental writing and an attention to recent British poets generally ignored in this country.

Since being eclectic is not always taken for a virtue, we would note that our eclecticism—besides simply reflecting personal ranges of appreciation—is based on an inability to believe that the history of, for instance, poetry can possibly be clear before the poems are written. It is not denying the importance of "movements", to insist that there is another importance in moving beside or apart from them. After all, there are many judgements, none of them the last.

We have, for the most part, printed Burning Deck publications on our own letterpress. In the beginning—we were graduate students in 1961—it seemed the only way to afford publishing anything at all and, in spite of the drudgery involved, it remains a source of satisfaction. We admire fine printing (under no illusion that ours is such) and admire any press that prints good work, even by mimeograph. Our own practice—a middle way—is to design and print things as well as we can (as fitting the care that has gone into the writing), in permanent form, but at a price that will not keep them on closed shelves.

The reader of the bibliography at the end of this volume will discover that Burning Deck has made two changes of address—from Ann Arbor to Durham, Connecticut, in 1964 and from there to Providence in 1968—the result, in both cases, of a new job for one or the other editor. It will also be clear that in the last half of the seventies the press's output increased considerably. These increases were made possible by grants from the National Endowment for the Arts and from the Rhode Island Council on the Arts, to both of which we are grateful, and of whose help we believe we have made good use.

The present selection is more or less chronological, beginning with poems from our first publication, *The Wolgamot Interstice,* and from the magazine. These, along with many of the pamphlets, are long out of print. We were unable to find passages sufficiently self-contained to excerpt from some works, such as Charles Hine's *Wild Indians,* Anthony Barnett's *Poem About Music,* or Jaimy Gordon's novella, *Circumspections from an Equestrian Statue.* Fortunately, all these are still available.

The selections, with the accompanying bibliography—complete through 1981—are meant to suggest what we have managed in twenty years of inconsistent desire, intermittent effort, and continual distraction. If we go another twenty, all we guarantee is that we will have something more, perhaps different, to show.

K. & R. W.

anthology

ooo

JOHN HEATH-STUBBS

ooo

NOT BEING OEDIPUS

Not being Oedipus he did not question the Sphinx
Nor allow it to question him. He thought it expedient
To make friends and try to influence it.
In this he entirely succeeded,

And continued his journey to Thebes. The abominable thing
Now tame as a kitten (though he was not unaware
That its destructive claws were merely sheathed)
Lolloped along beside him—

To the consternation of the Reception Committee.
It posed a nice problem: he had certainly overcome
But not destroyed the creature—was he or was he not
Entitled to the hand of the Princess

Dowager Jocasta. Not being Oedipus
He saw it as a problem too. For frankly he was not
By natural inclination at all attracted to her.
The question was soon solved—

Solved itself, you might say; for while they argued
The hungry Sphinx, which had not been fed all day,
Sneaked off unobserved, penetrated the royal apartments,
And softly consumed the lady.

So he ascended the important throne of Cadmus,
Beginning a distinguished and uneventful reign.
Celibate, he had nothing to fear from ambitious sons;
Although he was lonely at nights,

With only the Sphinx curled up on his eiderdown.
Its body exuded a sort of unearthly warmth
(Though in fact cold-blooded) but its capacity
For affection was strictly limited.

Granted, after his death it was inconsolable,
And froze into its own stone effigy
Upon his tomb. But this was self-love, really—
It felt it had failed in its mission.

While Thebes, by common consent of the people, adopted
His extremely liberal and reasonable constitution,
Which should have enshrined his name—but, not being
    Oedipus,
It vanished from history, as from legend.

D. C. HOPE

o   oo

OBLIVION

From any action there survive,
by spontaneous ignorance,
those few who spent their sketched-in lives
in converse that barely touched them,
killing as giddy children dance,
all innocent of strokes that can
bleed white, efface, oblivion.

Still in archaic carvings, solemn
masters fight by twos—suspended,
close, at death's pink and spongy edge:

their art is sweet, their taste for blood,
cut by the savor of knowledge.

ROBERT CREELEY

OO   O

THE LION AND THE DOG

Let who will think of what they will.
If the mind is made up, like an animal,
a lion to be suffered, a dog to pat,
action follows without conclusion

till all is stopped. The conclusion
is not variable, it is. From that
which was, then it, the lion if it is,
or dog, if it is, is not. It has

died to who thought of it, but comes
again there, to wherever that mind was,
or place, or circumstance being compound
of place, and time, now waiting but patient.

And all that is difficult, but difficult
not to think of, saying, lion, dog, thinking,
thinking patience, as an occasion of these,
but never having known them. But they come,

just as they came once, he thought, he
gave them each all that they were, lion,
but a word merely, and only a dog of sound.
All die equally. The mind is only there,

but here he is, thinking of them. They
are patient. What do they know? They know
nothing. They are not but as he thought.
But he knows nothing who thinks. They are.

DOROTHY DONNELLY

o   o   o

KUDZU

That famed and feigning genie
who rose up out of the vase
    the fisherman found,
    and swelled from a wisp
to a massive monster of mist
    that reached the clouds
and covered half a sea

has a real rival in the kudzu
which pulls itself out of itself
    like bushels of silk
    from a hat, a vine
whose magic-beanstalk climb
    is as strange, though a fact,
as the fake rope-act of the Hindu.

From a pinpoint start it spreads
right up to the roof—on the scale
    of an ostrich hatched
    from an aphid's egg;
and though it hasn't a leg
    to stand on, it stands
twenty feet over our heads.

Equipped for competitive action,
this plant comes armed, is rough,
 all saw-teeth, prickles,
 and runners with rasps
for feet with which it grasps,
 gropes, and shoves
its way by serpentine traction.

It has, if balked of rising,
tricks up its sleeve: it will crawl,
 clutch at a straw,
 rear like a snake
scouting for prey, then strike,
 and curl in its coils
some Laocoon doomed to strangling.

But if those tentacle tendrils
find tall things to cling to, up
 go the leaves, high, wide,
 and as handsome as
the Corinthian acanthus,
 advancing two
by two, alike as stencils.

Growing less, it grows more, begets
begetters. What genie could match it,
 this kudzu which conjures
 by natural acts
the hundreds of green steeple-jacks,
 waiting their turn
to climb, that pack its pockets?

LOUIS ZUKOFSKY

o   oo

THE WAYS

The wakes that boats make
and after they are out of sight
the ways they have made in water:
loops, straight paths,
to do with mirror-like,
tides, the clouds the deep day blue
of the unclouded parts of the sky,
currents, gray sevens or darker shadows
against lighter in and out weaving
of mercurial vanishing eights,
or imaginably sights
instantaneously a duration and sun,
and the leaping silver
as of rain-pelted nipples
of the water itself.

PRETTY

Look down out how pretty
the street's trees' evening green
with the day's with them
on globular lights no Hesperides
was has fruit more lemony
orangey cherryie honeydew melon white
like several white sports cars
turned the corner no peachier
headlights blaze in dark sides
of a row of cars
half-parked on the sidewalk
while for once nowhere here
fruits smell sing the mechanics

ROBERT DUNCAN

○   ○ ○

SONNERIES OF THE ROSE CROSS
Erik Satie whose thought returns
TO HIS MASTER SAR PELADAN

Everywhere the bells
sound
accumulating
a steady chime

 that gives

time into the depths of time.

Précieusement, he directs
the puzzled novitiate.
Does he mean
 affectedly?

 We look up to see
the silly magus administer
 with exqwisite
gestures mysterious measures

 in which

he sleeps within the hill of changing chords,

 sonorous ringings,

runes of the piano toward
Mont Segur reveald thru rites

 as the music's lure.

*

The eye
　　whose gilt-flakes gleam in whose grey
follows
　　iris-radiant purple and azure
　　　　emerald limnd

　　　　wand of the peacock-angel, one
of the many-eyed specter
　　upward.

　　　　Précieusement!

　　Fakes of his glory

God ever coming into His being

　　shows.

*

Sar Péladan
silly old man

I have prepared for you
sequences of a cathedral in blue,

holy ghostly musical
columns and staind-glass windows

O Magister,
because we were fond of beauty, here

a Sainte-Chapelle of the mystic rose,
an odor released in the notes changing.

Through the obedient priest at the piano
I have prepared

instructions
for the young knight's

tapers and insurrections.

*

There must now be
too too much of beauty in this beauty.

For the spectator
there is no trial of his trust,

no contest in the ritual,
without that specter

hand infatuate of the rose
preciously, with precious care,

the rapt poseur, intent,
before the altar

of Psyche, or butterfly-wingd
Iris—some made-up

some pretend
mystery of the too divine

the Master pretends to.
Don't laugh.

Is there a place for such posing
to be containd? for even

fakes of God to touch
some youthful trembling at the edge of God?

The Gothic has spoils in thought,
an almost girlish appearance of

solemn airs

the music takes.

LEROI JONES

O   OO

CROW JANE

> Crow Jane, Crow Jane, don't hold your head so high,
> You realize, baby, you got to lay down and die.
> —Mississippi Joe Williams

For Crow Jane

(Mama Death.

For dawn, wind
off the river. Wind
and light, from
the lady's hand. Cold
stuff, placed against
strong man's lips. Young gigolos
of the 3rd estate. Young ruffians
without no homes. The wealth
is translated, corrected, a
dark process, like thought, tho
it provide a landscape
with golden domes.
                          'Your people

without love.' And life
rots them. Makes a silence
blankness in every space
flesh thought to be. (First light,
is dawn. Cold stuff
to tempt a lover. Old lady
of flaking eyes. Moon lady
of useless thighs.

Crow Jane's Manner

            Is some pilgrimage
to thought. Where she goes, in fairness,
'nobody knows'. And then, without love,
returns to those wrinkled stomachs
ragged bellies of young ladies
gone with seed. Crow
will not have. Dead virgin
of the mind's echo. Dead lady
of thinking, back now, without
the creak of memory.
            Field is yellow. Fils dead
(Me, the last . . . black lip hung
in dawn's grey wind. The last,
for love, a taker, took my kin.

Crow. Crow. Where
you leave my
other boys?

Crow Jane in High Society

                        (Wipes
her nose
on the draperies. Spills drinks
fondles another man's
life. She is looking
for alternatives. Openings
where she can lay all
this greasy talk
on somebody. Me, once. Now
I am her teller.
                         (And I tell
her symbols as the grey movement
of clouds. Leave
grey movements
of clouds. Leave, always,
more.

Where is she? That she
moves without light. Even
in our halls. Even with
our laughter, lies, dead drunk
in a slouch hat famous king.
                               Where?
To come on so.

Crow Jane The Crook

Of the night
of the rain, she
reigned, reined, her
fat whores and horse.

(A cloud burst,
and wet us. The mountain
split, and burned us. We thought
we were done.

                             Jane.
Wet lady of no image. We
thought, you had left us. Dark
lady, of constant promise. We thought
you had gone.

2 My heart is cast in bitter
metal. Condiments, spices
all the frustration of earth,
that has so much more desire

than resolution. Want than pleasure.
Oh, Jane. (Her boat bumps at the ragged
shore. Soul of the ocean, go out, return.
Oh, Jane, we thought you had gone.

The Dead Lady Canonized

                                       (A thread

of meaning. Meaning light. The quick
response. To breath, or the virgins
sick odor against the night.

                                       (A trail

of objects. Dead nouns, rotted faces
propose the night's image. Erect
for that lady, a grave of her own.

                                     (The stem

of the morning, sets itself, on
each window (of thought, where it
goes. The lady is dead, may the Gods,

                                    (those others

beg our forgiveness. And Damballah, kind father,
sew up
her bleeding hole.

VALERIE WORTH

OO   O

DISEASED ELMS

Hearing, day to day, of how we die,
We could begin to mark a map with pins:
Shapes of towns or of the larger lands
Would soon show mottled, or, by chance, some clusters
Might collect, but hardly lines or rows.

Even in war, death scatters its ranks;
The executed, kept to twos or threes
Ranged briefly by a wall, are quick to buckle;
But the elms that stand along this road
Are marked for one slow geometric fall.

The street slopes down; looking from the top
We see their rows converge: some perfect planting
Years ago keeps order even now
And in that order they decline, too struck
For healing, thus arranged in upright graves.

We cannot look ahead to what will be
A barren street—their shade is steady still,
Though thinner than last year's; they multiply
Their branches and their leaves quite well, so far,
And will be felled before their sap is gone.

Still, they stand as calm as saplings, proud
As if assault by insect or by men
Meant nothing; their affair is with the sun
And not with saw or cable, jaw or germ;
Their work is all for water and warm air.

Although our houses take their stance like trees
Along the many roads we have made straight—
I can mark towns that grow as if for battle,
Yard along yard, street defending street—
To change that map would be a coward's gesture:

Our pinpricks grow from time and not location.
Still, if the patterns of all lives, not deaths,
Be shown (and, in the end, lives grow to deaths,
Close the spaces up) we can conceive
Geometry enough to square the globe.

But then to mourn the elms is not to die;
To cut them and forget the shade they cast,
A trifle to one generation—none
Keeps track, not even ailing grandfathers
Have seen that graves are mustering their rolls,

Have seen the houses termite-eaten, ill
As any bark, the mothers drawn to death,
The children blighted in their cradle-boles:
Their occupation is not yet with earth
But with warm air, and sun, and water, still.

ROBERT KELLY

o   oo

A CRAFT

sunflowers turn to ripe
the milk green stalks are coarse

a shadow makes
three of me
across the grass
bent in the
direction you vanished in

everything is about time

I would draw with gold ink
the picture of your secret place
the cobbled courtyard where you walk
around & around the fountain
late in sun

> the city's too hot
> I will live
> out of town
> a hollow place
> defined by what it's not

& will make gold ink

> *Encaustum aureum:*
> exhibit
> 2 measures florets of saffron
> in
> 12 measures water
> which bring to boil &
> while it cools bring to it
> the same weight of oil of flax
> 2 measures powdered gold
>
> mix well

& still fail the picture

PHILIP LEVINE

o   o   o

THE ONE-EYED KING

At last I found and faced you there;
My two eyes fixed a steady eye
In the kingdom of necessity.
Heavy with the true despair

That comes from finding what you are,
I bowed and said *My God* to you,
And you bowed as you lately do
And held your piece. It's almost here —

The day on which our guts will billow
Like mattress stuffing, our lungs blow
Like ashes, and the shapes go —
So rest awhile on the pillow

Of this tired thigh, rest and begin
To shrivel back where you began,
Where some old idiot said the man
In all his glory sheds this skin.

CHRISTOPHER MIDDLETON

o   o   o

From PATAXANADU

The firmamental rand of highways that encases the scaly vagrant of huge liege, is the hopscotch for the maintenance of its ingratitudes.

On its ricochets the comminuted sump has been and dented.

From them the standstills rinse, and tossing them vacillate.

By the manuls*, even this rand, the natatory limbo and bull's eye of the vagrant, is but impecuniously knifed.

Its hierocratic Aryans are too often heroized by missionaries and closets from uncropped swaggerers, which foetor hatches (county or cure, to pelt).

To the mullet below, these missionaries appear now as the dapper hat-tricks of ternary agates, on which none may intone with impudence;

and now all aghast, with colons not their own, they are gasped at as the splanchic paintresses of haplessness and pousse-cafe.

But in all afterthoughts there has been a foetor which, mauling and sopping the rissoles of the vagrant at the fondnesses of its funniest impudent falbalas, has learned that the sounds must be far more hieratic and inviting —

---

*A small, wild, Tibetan, Mongolian, or Siberian cat, with grey fur and black stripes.

a foetor that even in the Lesbian strata has destroyed electrons which neither the vagrant himself nor the surpassing motorists construed or could supervise.

How and whence to these thoraxes, these strong posses, the artistic viscidity, the intrinsic knock-out may fierily supervene, can be learned only by the face.

I might ooze to the querist the woodwool with which Plotinus supplants nationalists, to announce a Silurian diet:

Should anyone interpellate them, how they wolf, if gorily they volley to liquate and spank, they will repine that it

"behoves thee not to dispossess us with interpreters, but to underreckon in sign manuals, even as we are signable, and wolf without woodwool."

ALAN SONDHEIM

o   oo

BIAFRA

+ + + erminate marks predeterminate ma + + + -------- +

warm, warm fire! the burned log! the*
changed position! poker! burned on o
ne side, then on the other! charing,
burning, covered with thick black as

+ + + ----------------- + + +
h, turning to heat and light!
]]]]]]]
]]]]]]
]]]]]
poem of biafran elements.
is this a poem.
i am reading Ibo folksong:
poem of biafran elements. from an ** *new po
other poem: "Yeke omo mi (do not   sition
cry my child)" I am reading Biafr
an Elements. Refrain: warm, warm
fire° it begins°to°bu°°r_____, ch
ars, covered with thick black ash
, on the other .))))To be written out by the reader, ** *n
ending two inches from page bottom, one from the t ew po
op. strike out words "left over." use them   sitio
                                                     n

1.write a poem 'biafran elements.'
2.do 1 using your own words entirely.
3.do 2 using your own predetermined marks.* * * new po
sition
word meaning of poem when completed: you ha
ve altered sounds; noise; etc. & reworked t
he poem.   *THE BIAFRAN ELEMENTS:*

1.where is Biafra?
2.what is the extent of its agricultural se
lf sufficiency?
3.what are the conditions of its airstrips?

These are °content questions.° Designate
them "C1," "C2," "C3." Then, finally, th
is question:

4. Do C1, C2, C3 belong within the
predeterminate marks?

PEYTON HOUSTON

o   o   o

THE HOTEL

Of the things chosen we
Have only these
Left now, yet possessing
Is only half of it, so why
Should complaint be made
To a careless and surly
Management?

The other half of it
Is more difficult to explain.
It is that
The things unchosen, neglected,
Rejected,
Somehow come back to one
With a luminosity that takes
Everything into itself. So we see
Choosing
Is only partly
Losing.

Thus in this hotel
The room and the view are not of the best but sometimes
I can see
Rows and rows of bright
Splendid possible
Landscapes, horizons, real
Worlds.

THINGS OF THE UNEXPECTED

1

There is never the thing we
Expect: God comes in the side
Door or up from the cellar. I
Saw today two red
Leaves blowing about in the wind, playing
Together as if they were
Puppies and it was
Ridiculous I was so
Happy.

2

The other part of it,
Conversely,
Darkness also uses sudden ingress:
My friend driving at night hit head-on
By a drunken driver in the wrong lane.

3

In the fun house
The jets blow
The skirts lift
The walls fall in on you
Out of them come crocodiles, butterflies,
Spiders, seraphim.

X. J. KENNEDY

o   o   o

BULSH

in memoriam: Alfred Jarry

1

Saint Bulsh bears gifts to dying paupers' hovels:
'*You lazy fuckers! hit these picks and shovels!*'

2

Bulsh in the desert prays, and camels bawl:
'*Head for the hills before he humps us all!*'

3

If visions of delight goad Bulsh, he'll beat
His breast; and if they goad him twice, his meat.

4

Hot from the hock shop Blush gloats. At a loss,
The devout have to skip four Stations of the Cross.

5

Before Bulsh kisses lepers' sores, his smile
He straightens, and his flattering profile.

6

With nickel poised to gong the beggar's pot
Bulsh waves the crew in for a zoom-up shot.

7   Bulsh's motto

Bugger the waif and screw old age unless
You're covered on prime time by CBS.

8

When Bulsh clears his throat to preach, falls a great hush,
The whole cathedral emptied in one flush.

9

Why does Bulsh laugh like some bad child of Belloc's?
He's won first grabs at Saint Swinessa's relics.

10

Suffer our little Brother Lark to come,
Leers Bulsh, with open cookbook under thumb.

11

'For penance, buster, smell me breaking wind!'—
Lately in Bulsh's parish none has sinned.

12

Plump girls stay pasted fast to Bulsh's slat,
Old bony ones he shrives in no time flat.

13

When grave Bulsh counsels girls about to be brides,
In the dim booth he hoots and slaps his sides.

14

Wise nuns at Mass keep bulldogs in their pew
Lest Bulsh's fingers play the Wandering Jew.

15

Young matrons pray, 'Saint Bulsh, man, get me pregnant!'
(His device: testicles, with penis regnant.)

16 *Bulsh, hearing St. Matthew*
     on publicans and sinners

I shouldn't bitch, I'm just one of the sheep,
But, Jesus Christ! the company you keep!

17

On old Skull Hill, Bulsh hollered up the Cross:
'Want me to spell you for a minute, boss?'

18

'What? Me rat on our Savior? Up your ass!
That'll be FORTY dracks, plus lunch and gas.'

19

Bulsh spies the tired step of the old Pope.
Within his breast quickens a certain hope.

20

Bulsh on the crapper thinks: What could be sweeter
Than squatter's access to the throne of Peter?

21   *Bulsh to the nuns*

Go buzz off, sisters, no more hosts to bake.
I fed one to a nigger by mistake.

22   *Satan on the mountaintop*

Why in Hell not adore me, Bulsh, my pretty?
You do it to me, I'll take Jersey City.

23   *Satan again*

I'll net the big trout yet. One of my ploys
Is dangling Bulsh pink wriggling altar boys.

24   *Bulsh's* carpe diem

Almighty God's a patient elevator.
Drink and fuck now, and be assumpted later.

25

When Bulsh found out he hadn't long to live
He fell to giving God more to forgive.

26   *Satan again*

What, Bulsh got extreme unction? Bless it! Foiled!
Slippery as eels he is, and always oiled.

27   *Bulsh lays a fat one*

High noon grows ominous, hard gravemounds heave
And, caught off balance, Doubting Toms believe.

28

On Resurrection morn it sore surprised
Bulsh to stand up and go unrecognized.

CHRISTOPHER MIDDLETON

o o o

THE FOSSIL FISH

1 village quote idiot unquote
look a walking often takes
long at you

    stops & slow hows
    he come through

      screwy? clutched in
his one scrotum hand the other
crumpled hugs a fingering book

2   them squads in
  helmets
      burning
    the dragonfly's eyeballs
  out
is just ants

3   & silver eggs on stems
      be nobbut topknots
of a grass — ah savage head
    see them caught
      nodding in the wind launch your airy
hundredfold
      parabolas of seeing

4   ivy around the capstone
starts to fizz:
early snailhorns are
sounding the systems
of their space

5   shorts white
at the sharp angle of
trim bronze legs
to a melon balanced
in one palm she subtends her
equilateral nose
deepening the hidden
rose of that sphere
between cone & cone

6   rock & bough
tumbled over slammed against
pluck out their fillets
of necessary flesh
mad pleasure
for once to bleed
on a hill groaning
with apricot trees

7   inside the shell, fields:
               listen, lavender, wheat
       behind it, blue
          mountain behind
        the wheat, the sun
     over the mountain, curving
         up, the wave murmur: it
        won't fall

8   storing its times
    the body
    learns weightlessness

    space be skin
    limit
    my flesh of lightning

9   toad
    crawls
    up
    boulders
    always
    dragging
    his
    ughs!

10   a place ribbed with quartz between
        soaring
            rock wings here the wind
    swivels crashing sucked
            back into its helix
        luminous flesh in which
          embedded far below beyond
            float mountains little
    mossy tuffets

11 feeling the leaf
    a tree
    wrote
    spine
    longwise it is not
    chinese but crinkles

12 calm in the face of nature

     fearful in the face of nature

    maggot, neither, holes
      up in a peach

13 to please a nymph
      sip at her spring
    so her true voice told
      first a far cry
    now sharper breaths
      moisten this rosy moss
    & soon for sure
      she will be coming

14   coming also his long gusts tell me
the wind a river he roars
          in pine trees pounding walls of rock
      to destroy he scatters to build

speech a silver breath & seed once he scooped
      a whole man from a cave
         flicked him away
like an eyeball

        with twisted clay
trumpets at dawn we call for him hopeless
      on the mountain

      he floats in the crested ocean eastward
     blue cattle waiting to drink
the first torrent of rays

      how else from his flowering
chiselled hollows
      could these bee snouts tap our honey

15   the fossil fish
  hides in time
for now it is the season

     & all the hunters come
  with long clean rifles

(Vaucluse: July–September 1969)

CARL MORSE

BEDBUGS

In my sleep I slap
The mattress flowers they
Are biting like a million tiny
Dreams a million
Boats are sinking
It is sunny
Roll raise shiver
Capsize slip
The sea receiving
As a scabbard
Swords a drinking
Swarm in silence
Or a sky of hiving bees
The spiral
It is sunny hum a million
Boats are sinking I am dying
Somehow calmly on a dry deck
That has kept its keel but slowly floods
Without having clasped the fingers of my friend.
Bedbugs suck blood,
Survive for years unnourished,
And smell horrible when crushed.
Their eggs are indestructible.

'JOURD'WEE

'Jourd'wee je reconnais l'abysse.
Gouffre is a good word too, suggesting as it does,
"Swallowed by caves."
But l'abysse has slide,
Like falling in a dream,
With a hop at the beginning.

Whoever says the BMT is Hell does not lie through his teeth.
It is a very Babel, full of knives,
And you can stop at Goya, stumps of torsos anywhere.
I wonder how cela s'arrange elsewhere.

Awkward as in Courbet, bovines gnaw a landscape grey.
"Do apples move?" [1]
Or only move the bowels of drunk cows?
Their puddles dot the pasture path.

Cows are the end of life,
Although boys also eat crab-apples.
Yet cows have horns to hook in the shirts
Of sun-burnt hayers,
And their udders sway at dusk.

But I am straying toward God,
And polarities of mal belie my pit.
Revenons aux mots.
Engloutement is wonderful,
Does not exist,[2] but does the job.

---

1. Cézanne, furious, to his wife, who moved while posing.
2. v. engloutissement.

47

WILLIAM BRONK

○   ○   ○

UTTERANCES

There are no near galaxies: this
as far as any, if not in terms of miles,
we know how meaningless miles are
in terms of miles. How far from me to you?

Everything is, almost in the utterance,
metaphor — as we measure miles, and miles
are meaningless, but we know what distance is:
unmeasurable. But there are distances.

THE UNBECOMING OF WANTED AND WANTER

It is hard to let go of the world even though
we know there is nothing to hold to and we have no hands
for the tenuous holding. Where it seems they may grip,
there is neither hand nor tangible burden: no hold.

We make out there is something lost in the letting go.
What loss? What loser? Want invented them.
Want says the loss is real. Want is real.
It is hard when we do not say what want wants.

THE LOSS OF GRASS, TREES, WATER

Here is the silence; it is everywhere.
Because it has always been, there is no time.

No need, then, to wait for the time:
it comes always in the sense it was always here.

Noise is here but never any sound.
We listen for sound; it is as if we were deaf.

Under the noise, silence is what we hear:
final, always, wherever. Silence is all.

Grass, I thought to keep you, would have stayed;
and you, trees, water, gone too.

TOM RYAN

o   o   o

From ENCEPHALOGEORGICS

1 farming is dangerous
     what you plant may grow
          on you

2 if my room
     were a meadow
     the books would
     be dung

4 acres
     the sectioned
     field
     in pain

6   Im
     mortal
     soil

10 con
        tour
      plow
          ing
      a
          void
      eros
          ion
      what
        a
      charge

15   i
      n
      s
      e
      c
      t
      s
      p
      r
      a
      y

17   our glass
      holds
      quicksand

19   cows
      are
      pigs

24   pasture
        ends
      if there
      is no
      point
      why this
      great
      needle
      in the hay
      stuck

JUDITH GROSSMAN

o   oo

FRIEZE

Two girls lean from the window out into the street. One, his cousin, scans the city for a suitor, promised to return for just one day. The other, a friend, watches as well, in a dress of complimentary color.

To spectators below, they appear as regular as night blooming flowers. Children point them out as crepe paper banners, recast into dye each evening, then flung out to dry.

In strolls the doctor. The elevator opens, reveals him, he is seated. He annexes chairs — in their midst he will reside for the morning, afternoon or evening of his visit.

Perpendicular to the doctor paces his mother. A man and woman who, if removed, would appear to be attending a ping pong tournament, follow her back and forth movement.

Guests loiter in the doorway, waiting their turn to arrive. They fret away the time by locating, among the available options, the particular tableau in which they thrive. (They litter the carpet with shreds of invitations. They aim spitballs at the tapestries. They threaten to organize. They seem pacified by four o'clock tea.) Some favor the window, others the circle of chairs; the remainder ape the mother's pace. New guests are invited on the average of one every clockwise; none will be received.

Children play beneath the colors in the window until called away. "In that house, a party is always going on," they convince one another.

Synopsis

Conflict, in contrast to *infatuation* (in this household — cyclical) is reciprocal:

Doctor	the *doctor* implicates his *mother's lover* in the theft of that love, the *lover,* the *doctor,* in the matter of the *first cousin.*
Doctor's first cousin	the *first cousin* loves the *doctor* in love with his *mother,* who adores the *lover* seated next to the *cousin* whom he (the lover) loves.
Doctor's mother	the *mother* fixes blame upon the *first cousin* for provocation of the *lover,* the *cousin* the *mother* for the preservation of the son's affection.
Doctor's mother's lover	

Additional Data on the Doctor

His eyes are fierce enough to paralyze a legion.

He shares his father's residence in order to sustain the source of money and leisure necessary for the pursuit of pure melancholia.

He solicits followers, converts, fellow sufferers in silence. He gains them on balconies, under beds, in closets, where he has driven them from friends and relatives after his arrival.

He seeks a place where love is passed from one to another, but never returned: a solid formation of scowls, grimaces and frowns.

Suddenly the doctor is summoned by love for his first cousin.

He prowls the rooms of sleeping bodies, running his hands over each, "Alert, arise, I've jumped the gates, guards, the sleeping dogs to find you; I've walked miles behind a cruising taxi—always a few kilometers ahead, testing its lights, horn, blaring radio music to accompany my pace. Finally it halted.

By the time I reached, the driver was slumped asleep in the back seat. I drove the rest of the way, parking across the street to confuse him. Up, before he starts off again."

For today the girls select puce/magenta against a grey/blue sky; for yesterday a celebration: sepia/pearl honoring a partial eclipse of the sun; tomorrow, ebony/coral — indigo/mauve? They ponder the scenery for pleasing harmonies of color. Bangles of lapis lazuli orbit their wrists: again and over, around and again, over and around. Their ears feel the flap of onyx earrings set in motion by the wind.

Each time the doctor disappears, they grieve. The two girls change to matching black. Children flee in terror to a distant playground. The mother bends forward and away in grief — if removed, would seem to occupy a rocking chair. The man and woman attend her motion.

(Various sound effects will be simulated: the recoil of a pistol, the friction of a fall, the last waver of a noosed one . . .)

During rains the two girls are perceived as peonies uprooted from the nonexistent window box. As soon as precipitation is felt merging with their bones, foresight borne from long exposure to the weather, they begin to scheme a blend of pink, red, and white.

He reappears, Huckleberry Finn arriving at his own funeral. He tiptoes from the elevator, is seated in the midst of his chairs —left, in his memory, as he had arranged them. A light veneer of dust has settled; he sneezes.

The two girls shed their black. The mother reactivates her pacing.

Each time he disappears, they will take up grieving—a diversion, a sabbatical, an outing, high adventure in their own house.

Those inside the room regard the girls as carefully tended fixtures. Until the day arrives, they will always block the window, shifting color only, producing like intervals of even modulated tones.

ROCHELLE OWENS

o   o   o

WILD-WOMAN & THE NATURE OF HORROR & LOVE

the glowing   the blue
broken   solid/earth   melting   I did
BEHOLD   the field of Sloth
       & eye
of GOD

the mental
soul cleansing
the body/& with a SWORD
purifying
the Awakening

the first is weight
& white crying sky
/the second is
hanging tongue &
joined fingers   & yellow crookedness

transform & Exalt!
force the slipping
S N A K E   the   beast
taste of darkness &
pure DISTORtion

how can you make the distinctions
/utter three sounds?

this bird
this wind
this now/
this pain
this passion/
this new-born
two pieces of
frog

this chunk of
stiff-necked barbaric
piss-pride!

        this wish for/
        virtue   when the song
  of wild-woman

  is the nature of horror
through Love

       .know me like the Sea.
O Beware!

PETER RILEY

OO   O

From STRANGE FAMILY

2 terms of
   shadow, the pillar of cloud
   flickers in my chest as a whole
   range of wish on the edge
   of the funnel "for you"
   a way of approach
   a movement of the eyelids
                                 as

   clear as daylight

   fresh as the star of

4 it is raining in my head
   it is urinating in my heart
   it descends
               like bribery in
   circus after circus
   till the lips swell
   and the knees disjoint
   it seeps
   down through
   all the strata of sense to
   where it touches
   the roots of a sneeze

     breaking the cycle

     glass wheel scattered faery on the road

5(a)   he makes the
                sign, of the
             wanderer, sigh of
          rain & coming up
             over the bridge
          the entry   a mode
             of thinking in
          tune, why not

5(b)   make it the
                      sight, of
                   winter, sort of
                pain & looking up
                   into the arch
                the entire air a node
                      to fast
                   en what to

6   intending to fall
          into the brightness
       bending to touch the leaf
       on the ground   the drop
             of moisture on the bank
       tending to force
             brightness into the soil
             touch of a finger

9   who can't trust this silence
       & won't have it for good news
       there is life and there is
       not & this isn't
       death but the halt
       in getting across   the
       steppe   to be taken
       taken

TERRY STOKES

o   o   o

UNMENTIONABLES

1 To speak as tho
   the wind had caught fire,
   spoiling a long picnic. You
   held her as if it had never rained
   on Sunday in any park
   you visited. The clouds barked
   in the blue sky; the clouds
   barked all that
   rotten night.

2 Bad Spanish cognac & trains going
   a thousand places at once. The travels
   that took us away, & then
   took us away. They are paging you
   again & you were nearly in Paris.
   The stars were Gouda cheese, & everybody was offering
   something. Nothing you could hold
   onto; nothing you could sink your teeth into.
   Surviving was a trait
   we learned, deftly, pinning
   someone to a stiff brick wall at night,
   & lifting the toe easily
   & busting up their crotch. The buildings
   were built; the buildings tumbled. Dirty sand;
   lousy construction. But the pay
   was low, & the safety regulations, minimal.
   & no one gave up.

3 If I get into my heart, I get into
    areas where only oblique images
    fester, pus up
    under the heat, the burning of
    small animals in my veins, clawing
    toward my heart, driven back
    downstream. Oh the rough weather,
    the tidal wave invisible until
    the tidal wave. He stands on the shore
    like a man standing on the shore
    waiting for the water to dissolve his eyes.

4 Sometimes it is called
    the last chance. A turtle
    on his back, checking out
    the wonders of sky, air.

POEM FOR VALENTINE'S DAY & INCOME TAX

At 8am I am given the fact
that we do not have enough dependents,
we will surely pay.

What's the matter with us,
have we lost a child someplace this year,
did he, she, it, roll out the glass door
of our car on some family outing, i.e., business
expense?

O. K., let's sit down calmly
& count the kids.
Zero. Something's missing.
"If you had a loss in a prior year which
may be carried over to 1970, you
should enter it as a *minus*."

I thought we had carried everything forward.

MARK STRAND

○　　　　　　　　○　　　　　　　　○

From THE SARGEANTVILLE NOTE BOOK

A man in Utah hates my work.
Do not disappoint him, Excellence.

When I am with you, I am two places at once.
When you are with me, you have just arrived
with a suitcase which you pack
with one hand and unpack with the other.

I am thinking of HB and RH and HM and SF
and WB and DJ as I sit reading HV on WS.

He told himself she no longer existed.
When he saw her in the street
he knew he had seen her somewhere,
but could not place himself.

What shall we do, Fine Line,
who stand between the poem and nothing?

The days are ahead
1,926,346 to 1,926,345.
Later the nights will catch up.

When X. was 37 he celebrated his 49th and 50th
birthdays to get them out of the way.

Take my side
and there will be nothing left of me.

NANCY CONDEE

o   ∞

THE RAPE OF SAINT EMAD

1   Saint Emad dreams of a stone.

2   Saint Emad dreams of Our Lady of Kazan, limping through this century on her one stone leg.

3   Saint Emad dreams she has been thrown into a stone prison and is kept alive by the Lord who appears to her in the form of a gull and feeds her tiny fish through the bars of her window.

4   Saint Emad dreams of Saint Liberata, the fishwife with the white beard hanging on a cross.

5   Saint Emad dreams of a woman with a white apron hanging her husband's shirts and hanging her husband and hanging.

6   Saint Emad dreams of a dancing bear with a clothesline around his neck and of the man in the bear suit dancing and of the bear dancing in the man in the bear suit.

7   Saint Emad dreams of the breed of men that works in shoe stores, savage as rabid bears and reserved as the tongue of a laced boot. Saint Emad enters the shoe store. She is trying to find boots for saints. Gulls enter with her. They buy silicone spray and leave. Suddenly the salesman at the other end of the store comes dashing towards her, tripping over small children and legs looking at themselves in little leg mirrors. Flushed and panting, he kneels down and places a box before Saint Emad. Lifting the lid, she sees a male shoe, flopping about and gasping like a fish out of water. Saint Emad tries to explain that this is not the kind of footwear she had in mind, but the man does not listen. Slowly, gently, he slips his hand under her heel.

ANDREW CROZIER

○　　　○　　○

From THE VEIL POEM

1 In the dark there is a fretwork
that reveals a lightness beside it, gradually
a tree stands out from the hedge and
the rest of the garden, the sky lightens
and bleeds off at the edges, quite sharp
but not definite, the blueness has the frequency
of space and there is nothing else but whatever
has brought this tree here, quite taut
but flowing smoothly through its changes
I know it again and again and see how
set in one place as it is and small and
fragile I cannot dominate it, in the dark
or with my eyelids closed it will score
my face. Along a bright corridor the way
turns or is transected and is lost
in shadow, framed by a black latticed screen
its light foreshortened, lacking
depth. There is no radiant source within
these walls, they hold the sunlight to
define their intricate arcing.

3 In nature everything, we suppose, connects up
with everything else, yet this garden
is no natural symbol but one of a series
a complex system displaying a process
which is its own symbol when the people
off the train come out their back doors
to potter about. They do this
at weekends or in the evening when it begins
to draw out, the struggle of what is light and

what dark seen thus to advantage in a
domestic, backyard setting. How nature
disguises herself, how like a woman, she has
turned from her solitary way, withholding
a unique gift of truth. For the hermetic
correspondence of forms hidden beneath appearance
we substitute the ideal market of ecology
gross and substantial. Though we would rob nature
of her profusion this arch the roof of the world
echoes prodigally down the corridor, its facings rendered
an exactly repeated tracery of magic in
cardinal numbers, at each diurnal arc
a hanging lamp mimics our sun.

4 Bend back the edges and pull what you see
into a circle. The ground you stand on
becomes an arc, the horizon another
each straight line swells out
leaving no single point at rest except
where the pitch of your very uprightness
bisects the projection of your focal plane.
Here at the centre of every intersecting circle
each infinite yet wholly itself
whichever way you turn a way is offered
for you to carry yourself, its knowledge
will inundate you unless it is held
along every inch of your skin, shaped as
the grace you make for yourself. The starlings
are all in place on the lawn, scattering
up and down for little things, they rise
in flight or plant their beaks into the earth.

RAY DIPALMA

∞   ○

COWBOY QUOTIENT AT THE CINEMA

How much jackal how much wolf

The japs almost took this one
but We with our faces like boiled pork

pulled it off

but the bank teller medic
got it in the back

it wasn't the first time
control of the world grew a nipple

COWBOY DEALS WITH SOCIAL CREDIT

What a fucking phenomenon!

A lot of well used
                 intelligently well used
surplus
money
      made this possible

and NOW   shortly thereafter
I'm shovelling snow

Seems tempting enough

(kazoo music here)

THE PURITY OF DIFFICULTY

I choose policy
to make ends meet
you have only the cashable
regrets and you are no
simpering jesuit

you are Cowboy
on the bare stage
you are refreshing
and humble the haphazard
steady huff huff and true

salute

and now *and now*
speeding to cover your
mouth with your elbow
because I am talking
you get the Idea

heat spirits precision
my friend and syllabus
my intense buffoon and glory
work heat poised and valiant
heat

salute!

PATRICK FETHERSTON

○　　　○
○

From HIS MANY AND HIMSELF

A thing
like a stone
goes on
in his head,
then drops
to the bottom
of the bodywell;
and the news he wants comes to him
from the threads in his flesh.
(Only last hidingday
by way
of the firmest nerve
he was shown how to be explicit.)
The news of feeling he wants comes to him.

= = =

In the fifties
hard and with honour he worked
and was emptied.
In the sixties
he was called posthaste
to some mockfront
by all the stimuli
and they scraped the bottom of the brothel
till the bottom of everything else was on top.
He hasn't properly tested
the seventies;
he's merely overrested them.

= = =

When his clock stops
it's a bad time;
or when there's no chronometry
in private at all;
or when he can't hear his pips.

= = =

What was that void he saw himself in
last night?
That was no void;
that was his plight.

= = =

Where was he
when the close lives went out?
Fitting in with death.

= = =

Why was it shocking:
the cross? the rood?
Because of the blood from his side.

= = =

Was his god love?
Well, he wore himself to a ghost
making the relics kissable
if not exactly palatable.

= = =

He's afraid
that, if he interrogates heaven,
it will rain a treat.

GEORGE HODGKINS

ooo

MEMORIES

I had no good reason to keep them,
being, as they were, used,
and certainly no idea
what I'd do with them ever,
if anything. Nevertheless,
I was greatly disturbed to find
last night, on counting them up,
they were not all there.

Not many were gone; more likely
a few had just slipped away:
Never having kept records (indeed
how *would* one record such things?)
I could not know for sure.

This has happened many times;
each time I get flustered
and each time comfort myself
with one that never gets away:

that a man can break a hologram
into, say, one hundred pieces
and with each piece produce an image
identical to the original,
though lacking somewhat in definition:
that a man needs all of the pieces
only for perfect resolution;
and even then, the image looks
sickly in color, and one
cannot see behind it.

IT TAKES TIME

It takes time,
you know, to reassemble
piece by piece
in a new place;
it takes time
and concentration
and more faith than
any one man should have.

The sun is not always
reassuring, sharp outlines
are not always
clarifying,
numbers do not
always add up.
Words frequently lead
to no answers.

And it takes time
to learn these things,
repeating them in sequence,
rearranging,
adding, subtracting,
filling in the blanks,
rearranging,
learning to ignore.

One can easily start
talking to oneself: I am
trying, have
patience, don't leave me.

FROM INCHES TO YARDS IN LINEAR FEET

With perseverance, blind devotion and
a modicum of technical skill, I knew,
many strange and mysterious things
can be learned.
                        One night
I walked, toe to heel, my right shoulder
always touching the wall, from one corner
of the house back to the same. I moved
the furniture as I went along, to save time
and to test my concentration.
                        Allowing
so many inches for each foot I sat
and calculated the interior circumference
of my house to be so many yards.

This knowledge, though not as useful
as I had hoped it would be,
has proved satisfying in ways
beyond my comprehension.

TIDYING UP

Under clear skies, on low-tide beaches, often
I see empty fiddler-crab shells left
decaying in the sand week after week.
I crush them religiously and pause
to marvel at the usefulness of poetry.

EDWIN HONIG

O   OO

PASSES FOR NICANOR PARRA

Imagine it's late and you've dreamed
there are no prisons anywhere
and no prisoners

A naked man comes up to test your smile
You cut him off
He returns smiling and in chains

Think of an old friend who died
Now turn in your chair and he's there
filling the doorway smiling

Rise and he walks straight towards you
Leave the room and he sits in your chair
waiting for you to enter smiling

Almost at ease with your wife and children
you sail out to an island together
At the helm you know the boat is sinking

You tell them   They try bailing out   Too late
You leap overboard   Gasping you turn
The boat sails by and they are cheering

Who sits so close when you try to rise
If only he'd move or stand up by himself
you'd spring to your feet in a flash

You make a last effort but it's no use
You turn at him to glare
He is weeping inconsolably

JACKSON MAC LOW

∞   ○

TRAIN ... 4 December 1964
I

Train rule atom intricate nitrogen.
Rule unusual leotard entropy.
Atom train ostrich might.
Intricate nitrogen train rule intricate casual atom train entropy.
Nitrogen intricate train rule ostrich genealogy entropy nitrogen.

Rule unusual leotard entropy.
Unusual nitrogen unusual social unusual atom leotard.
Leotard entropy ostrich train atom rule dies.
Entropy nitrogen train rule ostrich pope yearly.

Atom train ostrich might.
Train rule atom intricate nitrogen.
Ostrich social train rule intricate casual holiday.
Might intricate genealogy holiday train.

Intricate nitrogen train rule intricate casual atom train entropy.
Nitrogen intricate train rule ostrich genealogy entropy nitrogen.
Train rule atom intricate nitrogen.
Rule unusual leotard entropy.
Intricate nitrogen train rule intricate casual atom train entropy.
Casual atom social unusual atom leotard.
Atom train ostrich might.
Train rule atom intricate nitrogen.
Entropy nitrogen train rule ostrich pope yearly.

Nitrogen intricate train rule ostrich genealogy entropy nitrogen.
Intricate nitrogen train rule intricate casual atom train entropy.
Train rule atom intricate nitrogen.
Rule unusual leotard entropy.
Ostrich social train rule intricate casual holiday.
Genealogy entropy nitrogen entropy atom leotard ostrich
    genealogy yearly.
Entropy nitrogen train rule ostrich pope yearly.
Nitrogen intricate train rule ostrich genealogy entropy nitrogen.

II

Rule unusual leotard entropy.
Unusual nitrogen unusual social unusual atom leotard.
Leotard entropy ostrich train atom rule dies.
Entropy nitrogen train rule ostrich pope yearly.

Unusual nitrogen unusual social unusual atom leotard.
Nitrogen intricate train rule ostrich genealogy entropy nitrogen.
Unusual nitrogen unusual social unusual atom leotard.
Social ostrich casual intricate atom leotard.
Unusual nitrogen unusual social unusual atom leotard.
Atom train ostrich might.
Leotard entropy ostrich train atom rule dies.

Leotard entropy ostrich train atom rule dies.
Entropy nitrogen train rule ostrich pope yearly.
Ostrich social train rule intricate casual holiday.
Train rule atom intricate nitrogen.
Atom train ostrich might.
Rule unusual leotard entropy.
Dies intricate entropy social.

Entropy nitrogen train rule ostrich pope yearly.
Nitrogen intricate train rule ostrich genealogy entropy nitrogen.
Train rule atom intricate nitrogen.
Rule unusual leotard entropy.
Ostrich social train rule intricate casual holiday.
Pope ostrich pope entropy.
Yearly entropy atom rule leotard yearly.

III

Atom train ostrich might.
Train rule atom intricate nitrogen.
Ostrich social train rule intricate casual holiday.
Might intricate genealogy holiday train.

Train rule atom intricate nitrogen.
Rule unusual leotard entropy.
Atom train ostrich might.
Intricate nitrogen train rule intricate casual atom train entropy.
Nitrogen intricate train rule ostrich genealogy entropy nitrogen.

Ostrich social train rule intricate casual holiday.
Social ostrich casual intricate atom leotard.
Train rule atom intricate nitrogen.
Rule unusual leotard entropy.
Intricate nitrogen train rule intricate casual atom train entropy.
Casual atom social unusual atom leotard.
Holiday ostrich leotard intricate dies atom yearly.

Might intricate genealogy holiday train.
Intricate nitrogen train rule intricate casual atom train entropy.
Genealogy entropy nitrogen entropy atom leotard ostrich geneal-
    ogy yearly.
Holiday ostrich leotard intricate dies atom yearly.
Train rule atom intricate nitrogen.

IV

Intricate nitrogen train rule intricate casual atom train entropy.
Nitrogen intricate train rule ostrich genealogy entropy nitrogen.
Train rule atom intricate nitrogen.
Rule unusual leotard entropy.
Intricate nitrogen train rule intricate casual atom train entropy.
Casual atom social unusual atom leotard.
Atom train ostrich might.
Train rule atom intricate nitrogen.
Entropy nitrogen train rule ostrich pope yearly.

Nitrogen intricate train rule ostrich genealogy entropy nitrogen.
Intricate nitrogen train rule intricate casual atom train entropy.
Train rule atom intricate nitrogen.
Rule unusual leotard entropy.
Ostrich social train rule intricate casual holiday.
Genealogy entropy nitrogen entropy atom leotard ostrich geneal-
    ogy yearly.
Entropy nitrogen train rule ostrich pope yearly.
Nitrogen intricate train rule ostrich genealogy entropy nitrogen.

Train rule atom intricate nitrogen.
Rule unusual leotard entropy.
Atom train ostrich might.
Intricate nitrogen train rule intricate casual atom train entropy.
Nitrogen intricate train rule ostrich genealogy entropy nitrogen.

Rule unusual leotard entropy.
Unusual nitrogen unusual social unusual atom leotard.
Leotard entropy ostrich train atom rule dies.
Entropy nitrogen train rule ostrich pope yearly.

Intricate nitrogen train rule intricate casual atom train entropy.
Nitrogen intricate train rule ostrich genealogy entropy nitrogen.
Train rule atom intricate nitrogen.
Rule unusual leotard entropy.
Intricate nitrogen train rule intricate casual atom train entropy.
Casual atom social unusual atom leotard.
Atom train ostrich might.
Train rule atom intricate nitrogen.
Entropy nitrogen train rule ostrich pope yearly.

Casual atom social unusual atom leotard.
Atom train ostrich might.
Social ostrich casual intricate atom leotard.
Unusual nitrogen unusual social unusual atom leotard.
Atom train ostrich might.
Leotard entropy ostrich train atom rule dies.

Atom train ostrich might.
Train rule atom intricate nitrogen.
Ostrich social train rule intricate casual holiday.
Might intricate genealogy holiday train.

Train rule atom intricate nitrogen.
Rule unusual leotard entropy.
Atom train ostrich might.
Intricate nitrogen train rule intricate casual atom train entropy.
Nitrogen intricate train rule ostrich genealogy entropy nitrogen.

Entropy nitrogen train rule ostrich pope yearly.
Nitrogen intricate train rule ostrich genealogy entropy nitrogen.
Train rule atom intricate nitrogen.
Rule unusual leotard entropy.
Ostrich social train rule intricate casual holiday.
Pope ostrich pope entropy.
Yearly entropy atom rule leotard yearly.

V

Nitrogen intricate train rule ostrich genealogy entropy nitrogen.
Intricate nitrogen train rule intricate casual atom train entropy.
Train rule atom intricate nitrogen.
Rule unusual leotard entropy.
Ostrich social train rule intricate casual holiday.
Genealogy entropy nitrogen entropy atom leotard ostrich geneal-
ogy yearly.
Entropy nitrogen train rule ostrich pope yearly.
Nitrogen intricate train rule ostrich genealogy entropy nitrogen.

Intricate nitrogen train rule intricate casual atom train entropy.
Nitrogen intricate train rule ostrich genealogy entropy nitrogen.
Train rule atom intricate nitrogen.
Rule unusual leotard entropy.
Intricate nitrogen train rule intricate casual atom train entropy.
Casual atom social unusual atom leotard.
Atom train ostrich might.
Train rule atom intricate nitrogen.
Entropy nitrogen train rule ostrich pope yearly.

Train rule atom intricate nitrogen.
Rule unusual leotard entropy.
Atom train ostrich might.
Intricate nitrogen train rule intricate casual atom train entropy.
Nitrogen intricate train rule ostrich genealogy entropy nitrogen.

Rule unusual leotard entropy.
Unusual nitrogen unusual social unusual atom leotard.
Leotard entropy ostrich train atom rule dies.
Entropy nitrogen train rule ostrich pope yearly.

Ostrich social train rule intricate casual holiday.
Social ostrich casual intricate atom leotard.
Train rule atom intricate nitrogen.
Rule unusual leotard entropy.
Intricate nitrogen train rule intricate casual atom train entropy.
Casual atom social unusual atom leotard.
Holiday ostrich leotard intricate dies atom yearly.

Genealogy entropy nitrogen entropy atom leotard ostrich geneal-
ogy yearly.
Entropy nitrogen train rule ostrich pope yearly.
Nitrogen intricate train rule ostrich genealogy entropy nitrogen.
Entropy nitrogen train rule ostrich pope yearly.
Atom train ostrich might.
Leotard entropy ostrich train atom rule dies.
Ostrich social train rule intricate casual holiday.
Genealogy entropy nitrogen entropy atom leotard ostrich geneal-
ogy yearly.
Yearly entropy atom rule leotard yearly.

Entropy nitrogen train rule ostrich pope yearly.
Nitrogen intricate train rule ostrich genealogy entropy nitrogen.
Train rule atom intricate nitrogen.
Rule unusual leotard entropy.
Ostrich social train rule intricate casual holiday.
Pope ostrich pope entropy.
Yearly entropy atom rule leotard yearly.

Nitrogen intricate train rule ostrich genealogy entropy nitrogen.
Intricate nitrogen train rule intricate casual atom train entropy.
Train rule atom intricate nitrogen.
Rule unusual leotard entropy.
Ostrich social train rule intricate casual holiday.
Genealogy entropy nitrogen entropy atom leotard ostrich geneal-
ogy yearly.
Entropy nitrogen train rule ostrich pope yearly.
Nitrogen intricate train rule ostrich genealogy entropy nitrogen.

HARRY MATHEWS

o   o o

THE PLANISPHERE

for M. G.

Belated May warmth
In early November coolness,
When flowers sprang in the fields,
Where crystals flattened around a puddle,
When flowers collapsed:
You went straight from fleeting contentment,
Changing always as amazement,
In spite of their impermanence, disgorged their art
And impermanence laid bare its nature.
More bearable through familiarity,
More bearable in spite of unfamiliarity,
More bearable as the years teach,
Less bearable as the day obscures:
They would never change.
They might at once change intelligence of the other,
And ignorance of the other,
So perfect as to overcome
This hope, foster that dread, abandon
This fear, nourished through glooms of sexual sociability but
    then
Deprived, from maturity, of childhood;
Shattered, satisfied, with its occasional satisfactions
Shattered and satisfied, so that no dissatisfaction
Undid a fear more real than fear,
Made the hope more unreal as hope.
Cheerfulness took its place alongside eagerness;
Desperation replaced melancholy,

Lest the contentment, chopped up without satisfaction,
Freeze more darkly, without the ever-purer light into which,
On April 14th, you had risen.
They will be the darkness,
Darknesses blackening inside the hole. Summers—
Evaporation after November,
No snow after March—
Unveiled our minds as we waited,
Not because their quick-fastening brightness or its slow-pass-
    ing darkness condemned
Our unmoving darkness, your moving brightness;
But this summer dark and the old
Specks outside hard light over holes
Were no longer the impossibilities but that blankness opposite.
The lack of any reflection left differences in darkness,
Left no consistency, a tangle beyond voluntary dejection
(Essentials to sunlight and cave paintings)
But a simplicity without fogs or movies,
Ascetic persuasion so that no unrealized fear
Would cast off their improper unreality
As dream: its role of object
Had left untouched their uselessness with subjects.
Now you cannot cast an unknowing eye on things:
My own disappointment, your otherly satisfaction, my own
    satisfaction
Are no reasons now for your contentment.
However, I doubt this choice—and you doubt that indecision.
But I suspect that "choice"
Will be something old, and the closed door
Something new, extinguished, duller,
Although never shining less brightly than before.
Performing your life-to-be
And leaving my erstwhile life alone

In the future active tense
Is a fiction that allows me to pick
Facts (these have prevented you from removing
Fictions that forbid me to set
The hope and its resolution apart)
That were only observed in a present, never imagined from
the past,
Insolubility sinking nowhere, resolution floating nowhere.
Hesitantly, they had done worse by ceasing
To be repelled by exceptions, that is, by dying;
Living out an unconventional life
And dying in this unconventional manner, plunging on neither
with
Darkness under a still mass
Nor light on the still leaf.
You cannot think where you have no desire.
What I cannot touch and what I want
Was inside that exact restriction from a second,
But accessible to you.

RON SILLIMAN

o   o   o

verheard
versation

a day at

facial features

wind waits

st
aero

a plaid
etude

mmon

scow
coasts

SKY CHIEF

JAMES CAMP

○　　○　　　　　　　　　　○

A WINTRY FEVER

It's getting harder to remember the Thirties.
Public gestures are so replacing private embraces
That, thinking back, I can visualize Old Cactus Jack
Garner better than some of the sunburned faces

Of girls I once thought I wanted to marry.
It's all very sad, this furious emptying
Of musty privacy which will finally leave
Only tundras of starlit history.

I can say: "We stood this way on some day."
But which of three hundred and sixty-five?
Summer or winter? Mostly, I can't remember—
I can remember we were very much alive

One winter when all West Tennessee was glazed
With ice that crystalled the trees and caked the roofs.
Gullies in the creeks grew wider that year
When April came and the banks sloughed off.

That year my sister made love with my uncle,
And that year the Depression started to abate;
The year we burbled "Love in Bloom"
Was the year I really learned to love and hate.

And I stored memories in vaulted places
Along with scenes from movies, books and plays;
Then, gradually, I lost the bodies, then the faces;
Now only shadows move behind those glazed

Windows, as iced-over West Tennessee fades
Behind terraces where Ginger Rogers and Fred Astaire
Still dance, almost in focus, and only slowly recede
Into snow that sequins the starlit air.

THE BEAST IN THE JUNGLE

I went down to my mailbox
But I found the box was bare;
I came up to my kitchen,
There was no one waiting there;
I went into my bedroom;
Looked at the mirror on the wall;
The mirror stared right back and said,
"There's no one here at all."

Here pussy pussy pussy
Here pussy pussy pussy
Oh — — — — — — !

There's no beast in my jungle;
There's no tiger in my tank,
No big animals in my kingdom
And I don't know who to thank
For this awful terrible emptiness
That's crept into my soul
Cause I love everybody
And my heart is made of gold.

Quarters jingle in my pocket;
I got money in the bank;
I got some old hair in a locket,
But no tiger in my tank.
Each morning I go out and look
But there's no big animal in my trap;
My friends all say to sublimate,
But that's a lot of crap.

To find my self a tiger
I trekked out to the zoo;
The keeper said, "We've got those beasts,
But we've got none for you."

The keeper looked at me and said,
"Man, you've really got the shakes;
I'd get right home and get some sleep
And stay away from snakes."

I went into a movie house;
There were some big cats on the screen
But when I tried to reach for them
They vanished from the scene.
I went to the Office for the Poor;
They said, "Brother, have a chair;"
I said, "I just want my tiger."
And they chased me out of there.

I went to see my doctor;
He was on the seventh floor;
It was not the first trip I had made;
I was willing to make more.
Said," I cannot find my tiger."
He said, "Don't look so forlorn;
You've only lost your tiger;
I've lost my unicorn."

I said, "I've always been a good boy,
And I try to do what's right;
I vote the liberal ticket,
And I fight good freedom's fight
By writing to the New York Times,
But they never print a word;
I always try to groom myself
And never look absurd."

My doctor gave a glassy stare;
I was breaking down in tears.
He said, "I can find your tiger;
It will take me seven years."

I was staring at his glasses
When I guess I had a stroke.
As he took out his fountain pen
His Goddamn glasses broke.

I was back in my bedroom
Lying down on my bed.
My fingers still were quivering;
There was whirring in my head.
Small furry creatures
Were crawling in the air;
My wrists were ripped and bleeding;
Shattered glass was everywhere.

I suddenly saw a jungle gun
Shoot off its mouth like doom,
And then I fell asleep
And found a tiger in my room.
I heard its dying agonies;
Its eyes were glassy bright;
Then slowly like the Cheshire cat
They vanished in the night.

Here, pussy, pussy, pussy
Here, pussy, pussy, pussy
Oh — — — — — — !

There's no beast in my jungle
There's no tiger in my tank,
No big animals in my kingdom
And I don't know who to thank
For this awful terrible emptiness
That's crept into my soul
Cause I love everybody
And my heart is made of gold;
And my heart is made of gold.

JULY, LATE EVENING, NEWARK, NEW JERSEY

In an air-conditioned comb without honey
Designed by Mies Van der Rohe,
Whom I have never met but whose cold forms
I have now come intimately to know,
I read the private death of a public man,
Reach for my wallet to count my money,
And catch at the sting in death's undertow.

I have felt it before in Ann Arbor.
At a house numbered three thirteen
Death raged through the rusty screen,
Roared over the hardwood floor
Down the dusty, ragged carpet steps
And then once more took the night.
I felt it surge through the door
Long after I had put out the light.

Now it's timid. Just like a buddy,
It gives me a playful tug to join a game
I've always wanted to play but never dared;
The ending is, as always, the same.
I invent other games because I'm scared—
Maybe—of shopworn notions
Remembered from childhood like old brand names

Of unguents, ointments and oily lotions,
Medicines that never really cured anything,
But soothed the skin till the burning was over.
Now only burning stops the sting;
Instead of death I take pain, as a lover
Takes another woman when he's hot for it
And his real love wants an eternal vow.

AESTHETIC DISTANCES

Cake, ice-cream and soda pop,
Then . . . Bang! Pow!
And tiny wars in a twinkling of mirrors
Can make even a great commedia of errors
An echo in the sing-song gardens of delight.
And even gross indecencies on white subway walls
That couple "Judy fucks" with "Beverly loves Jim"
May, with perspective, when the writing has gone dim,
Seem quaint, fitting, and somehow finally all right,
And twenty centuries may
Make them pleasant as an excursion to Pompeii.
Forward or backward—out of time—
Anything but the glaring present,
The necessary indecent exposure.

IPPY GIZZI

o   o   o

From LETTERS TO PAULINE

Dear Mother

Do you think it is possible that life go on this way? Today I went out to milk the cows and I noticed two of their legs were missing. And the sky is such a furious gray, urinating on my face if you will, the most undisciplined and impudent organs of water so that later I am blamed for the puddles (partly because of the cowgrease they contain and partly because of the collection of ants, fingernails and underwear whose elastic waists are limp and undesirable even to a voyeur, all recognizably mine, floating free of my house and my gray curly brain after the rain, in and on the tops of the puddles.)

Mother, remember when I was young you put flour on my tongue. That flour, which made my teeth white and made the words float out of my mouth white, is still in me, making my blood an idiotic gravy you might be proud of, limiting my life, making me cough when others are laughing, making me bleed profusely at night with no solace save putting more flour on my tongue & feeling the flour mature inside me, a small fight then it dissolves into gas and my hands are perverted into cow's teats.

It is a remarkable thing mother that having been fed on flour all my life I have survived. I have gotten out of bed at sunrise, walked to the refrigerator, and seen the trail of flour blazing behind me near the wiry blue and pink lines of sunlight which make the floor seem electrified; I have, by stroke of luck, found the flour in my pockets on certain famished midnights in the corridors of boarding school dormitories where I stared at plants; I have puked flour, drunk it, given it to friends. On & on, the same flour which was once you, was once love, is now a substance I call life and there is nothing like it anywhere although I have seen something similar in Boston, Massachusetts.

STEPHEN SANDY

o   co

THE DIFFICULTY

1   —I don't care when
    it was made he said and
    left
    at the blade of day.
    —Why do you care
    so much
    who you are?
    You sit, wanting
    to know
    where a thing came from
    who made it,
    when. As if
    any of this
    information mattered. You
    see a collector's knowledge
    is dinky
    binary stuff. This
    concern is
    he said as
    that other that
    less articulate worry.

2   Once more the weather
    has turned the
    streets to saunas
    this morning
    radios warn heavy
    smog and
    outdoor exertion is
    classed as
    dangerous. And
    'by chance' or
    'therefore' the young men

thought to play
soccer again the same
game regardless
which causal
innuendo I pick to explain
its timing. Curious
meanings escape
me, I
dont know the schedule
or if there is one and
I cannot
speak with them.
For them
now
does this punishing
game there
signify? The worry
pulls like the sliding
heave
of perspective
where we are sucked
over
an edge, the abysmal
horizon in ver-
tigo falling away
when the plane
gains.

3 You see
said Daiji
I do not fuck
what
I see

—The rain
on the tiles
cuts off—

but what
I saw.

4 —This way you feel
about yourself
may remind you
not to
worry: who
made things
or how well.
The when the where
pinning
them down. The nick
of time.
To the victor
the spoils!
When you grow up
nothing
is personal.

5 The feel of
an undertow of
rituals
drawing the soul out
to the
sea to style
remains.

6 As touchmark
of his mastery he
could afford
to cherish his
body in the mirror.
Or leap
from bed to
shadowbox
the sun and run
before tea
before
anything calling
—Straight ahead!

BARTON LEVI ST.ARMAND

OO   O

EMILY DICKINSON READING WALT WHITMAN

I heard he was disgraceful, and he is!
The bearded rapist lurking in these folds
of velvet mossy-green, the Gift Book's gilt—
so innocent, so flowery, so genteel!
How could Father guess? No doubt he thinks
it is some girlish album full of gush
bought by his cast-iron railroad stock
(a striped adder nestling in the pile
of books he buys and begs me not to read).
What would Father do? He sits in state
below, assured the pious pages of
the *Sabbath Visitor* have nothing carnal in them
(dry as starched papyrus in the tomb),
while Emily receives a private caller.
"I mind how we lay in June, such a
                transparent summer morning;
You settled your head athwart my hips and gently
                turned over upon me.
And parted the shirt from my bosom-bone, and plunged your
                tongue to my barestript heart . . ."
Did Father feel like this when sanctified?
Signed, sealed, delivered by Christ's blizzard-kiss
to title in the company of Saints?
"These are the thoughts of all men in all ages . . .
They are not original with me . . ."
My hands grow stiff as death; physically I feel
as if the top of my head were taken off;
in spite of the squat air-tight's patent heat,
I turn so cold no fire can ever warm me.
Can this be poetry, or is it God
come for me as Father said he would?

96

"I am not an earth nor an adjunct of an earth,
I am the mate and companion of all people, all
                    just as immortal and fathomless as myself;
They do not know how immortal, but I know ..."
If this be "poison," then I down my dram!
"Who need be afraid of the merge?
Undrape .... you are not guilty to me, nor stale nor discarded,
I see through the broadcloth and gingham whether or no,
And am around, tenacious, acquisitive, tireless .... and
                    can never be shaken away ..."
What rosy fingers nibble at my gown?
". .voices veiled, and I remove the veil ..."
              /   /   /
The picket gate goes "chunk," and latches shut.
              /   /   /
Not my veil. No, that remains untouched;
inviolate, invisible, unassumed—
This *camerado* shall not penetrate
where sister, brother, lover drown alone
and even dread Jehovah skulks away,
cheated of the final nudity.
A poker stirs the white ash of the coals
as I consign these *Leaves* to leaves of flame,
without the Quaker poet's righteous wrath
(poor Whittier could not believe his eyes!).
"I depart as air ... I effuse my flesh in eddies and
                    drift it in lacy jags ..."
My web is cleansed. Dear Father will not know
the heathen suttee blazing in his house
destroying and preserving for that once
which is Eternity.
              Now I can write
again to Mr. Higginson who said
of Mr. Whitman it was no discredit
that he wrote his book but only that
he did not take and burn it afterwards.

KEITH WALDROP

○   ○
                                       ○

PROPOSITION I

Sunlight—yes. I
mean yes it's
there.

+

Things
separate. My
eyes smart.

+

Dark. Indefinite
sounding.

+

Two
knowledges: (1) not to
stumble, (2) not
to move.

+

Look on tip-
toe. Listen
horizontal,
breath held.

+

Under sixty watts. Write:

+

What
can I lure
here?

PROPOSITION II

Each grain of sand has its architecture, but
a desert displays the structure of the wind.

DAVID BALL

o   o   o

From THE GARBAGE POEMS

o accidie my accidie

of course my hairs are dragging too many disasters after them
a pacifist my head full of bombardments & burning
& accidie my *ça te coupe le souffle* accidie
a heavy burden
living with all the old enemies of man

listening to the news & the news is bad
my accidie stewing in the body's juices eager
to hear how others change what the body has built with pain
droppings the plants & their monkeys disappear
humus cover of the very earth does shrink

once wet & rich, this cover then forms laterite
which is a perfectly sterile crust. In
her feathered hair it's hard to even dream of enemies
of earth or of her hair when rats appear
& garbage. Those enemies are old

he heard about so torpor he could hardly breathe
& stinking. Pew. They fed on him he fed on them
just listening
they feed on me that once did gaily reek
now pewing sadly

the cracked earth laterized he dreamed
of water or a different fire
& the word for that is accidie o sir

have you seen my sloth or torpor
(the four elements be unruly servants)

---

kto tovo kto tovo
he wrote I thought it was a finnish bird
but no it meant burning
I think of this more than rolling in her peacock fan
song of that winning fire

that was long ago a question now of songs
& accidie confused reports from distant wars
turning the switch on found his rooms full of water
or was it the street from which came shouts & singing
uncontrollable flooding buzzing & sparks

rolling through the reddish water on the floor
fires outside or is it my room full of crackling
through the flooded street? cries banging smoke rising
from the city & its "millions of I I I's"
plus one while rolling in myself tasting & scratching

I think continually of that ancient fire

MICHAEL GIZZI

○   ○   ○

BIRD AS

So long as any body part
can articulate a bird
in flight
(say Ibis

remains
Every

Where a wing —
air

Eye of a man in love
with rivers

o there-
fore
wading

birds

And why not
If wings fit —

Run.

For your life —
a something soaring

You who've never flown
Except

to flutter

1 Dear V

    Just this
a note   on depression:

I have laid me down
in river silt

like the stone
always beside itself.

    Your dark bird
    swims overhead.

2   You say   you can't
fly
flat on your back
make that upright
recovery
necessary to being
at ease   w/ your
self

That's right
some nights
I dread
for this simple reason
they don't fly
for me even -
ings I sit up & tremble
at the far
end
making weird connections

3   Nothing really:
a blue
place.
You follow
a tunnel to
its own
tunnel.

Eyes in tow.
        The eyes in tow
        when a sudden
        turning birds
            your flesh
                        steps back
        the heart is
        a cliff
        & so it's always
        come to this
                        that
                        we are man
made to break.

4   If it's true:
              I am not my body
       then why not a bird
       the tree &
       the apple in it
       are successive
       objects
       necessarily essential
       and subject to
       fits of possession.

       Damn these arms the hands
       pushing air they won't let
       up they don't
       lift off.
       The desire to be bird
       like as to freeze
       my fingers glare light
       of ice & the air
           chimes:

                  youre ground dead
       its a specialty
                              rocks
                              dont fly   theyre
                              flown

                              butt   youre bittn
                              you dip
                              shit
                              all the same

5   Bird as a bird
is   what keeps a man
Keeps him up:
This keeps his heart
from falling
                down.
Bird as soul
or so it's said   sempiternal

            Long
                white
                    wing-
                        strides,
                    long
                white
                    scythe   lifts the air
knows
what goes in that long white head.

Know
that I don't.

6   *Is there*
good reason for
distinguishing
the sense in which
persons
may be said
to persist   OR
        thru time
w/ that in which
familiar physical
things
may be
said
to persist   thru time
lately
is it like rapport

else at once upon
the day this door
to the river rising
tells us:
we are two
of us—
2 fingers to
a fist
at a door
waiting for something more
unlikely, tho
a river's the sum
of its (each
of its) private
river parts

7 Dear V

    Just this—
a manic song

Please
do not think me.
I know
you will not.

    Say instead:
breath is man's animal
snowy egret is my emblem

    winter's home in
the winter body
nervous bird
in the act of
plumed bird   tall stalk   swallowing fish

        against a blue field

    + +

Parker's Point
Chester Connecticut
5/75

BARBARA GUEST

o   oo

From THE COUNTESS FROM MINNEAPOLIS

5 *RIVER ROAD STUDIO*

Separations begin with placement
that black organizes the ochre
    both earth colors,

Quietly the blanket assumes its shapes
as the grey day loops along leaving
an edge (turned like leaves into something else),

Absolutes simmer as primary colors
and everyone gropes toward black
where it is believed the strength lingers.

I make a sketch from your window
the rain so prominent earlier
now hesitates and retreats,

We find bicycles natural
under this sky composed of notes,

Then ribbons, they make noises
rushing up and down the depots
at the blur exchanging
its web for a highway.

Quartets the quartets
are really bricks and we are
careful to replace them
until they are truly quartets.

Although Paris has only one river, the Seine, this river behaves perfectly reasonably within the city limits, or arrondissements, approaching the isles with a courtliness and depositing its burdens with a verve one used to associate with the beret. A manner thus is maintained by the Seine which we define as raison d'être or Steak Diane or the French way of looking at things, sometimes it is true through a pigeonhole. Let's say neither New Yorkers nor Parisians are inclined to "river worship." Certainly they are appreciative of the uses commercial and aesthetic of a river, yet neither is inclined to "go overboard" on the subject. Nothing at all here Oriental or Indian in that respect, or Hungarian either.

When I come to the subject of Minneapolis and its posture on the Mississippi, a confusion like a drought descends upon me. Minneapolis persistently nagged by the unreasonable river that both gladdens and disturbs her heart. I may become convinced that the only way to survive a long, unsettling, barren Minnesota winter is to sit in a hut by the log fire and looking past the tears of confusion and loneliness falling down my pinched and overheated cheeks study, chew, harry a map of Minneapolis. Thus one might survive until spring.

The following winter I would exact from my tree chopping, whiskey thawing, sullen recounting of woes active and mystical, the labor of studying the Mississippi River. Her windings, divagations, idiosyncracies, bridges, dredgings, falls, destructions which yearly drive a mortal to the furthest limits of that angst called despair triumphed over by a northern people only through the spiritual suicide of its artists.

12 PRAIRIE HOUSES

Unreasonable lenses refract the
sensitive rabbit holes, mole dwellings and snake
climes where twist burrow and sneeze
a native species

into houses

corresponding to hemispheric requests
of flatness

euphemistically, sentimentally
termed prairie.

On the earth exerting a wilful pressure

something like a stethoscope against the breast

only permanent.

Selective engineering architectural submissiveness
and rendering of necessity in regard to height,
eschewment of climate exposure, elemental
            understandings,
constructive adjustments to vale and storm

historical reconstruction of early earthworks

and admiration

for later even oriental modelling

for a glimpse of baronial burdening
we see it in the rafters and the staircase heaviness
a surprise yet acting as ballast surely

the heavens strike hard on prairies.

Regard its hard-mouthed houses with their
robust nipples the gossamer hair.

21 "This street reminds me of scarceness, even loss like searching for hen's teeth in the rain," murmured the Countess to herself as she picked her way slowly down Hennepin Avenue. "I feel frightfully sad somehow and truly lost. I wish I had a glass of sherry right now, only that would never do. I mean I couldn't drink it here on the corner. Look at that gutter. So muddy. The wind's from the Southeast which should mean . . . I never know what it means. The prairies confuse me so. Perhaps Liv will have a hot bath ready when I finally reach home. That and the new frock from New York with the twin reveres. I wonder how reveres shall look on top of mutton sleeves. There's venison for supper. And the St. Louis Dispatch with luck should have arrived." The Countess hesitated for a moment as the sidewalk drifted into dirt and her grey eyes filled with dust.

25 The further exoticism of reading a British novel while visiting Duluth. The Countess usually "tucked one into her dressing case" when preparing for a visit to one of Theodoric's relations. The excitement of the Lake precipitated an unconscious association with former boating parties when she had been younger and, alas, inhabited a narrower world.

"Rather like reading of the River Niger while dining alone in New York," sympathized her cousin, Glanville.

34 And still she said,
    walking toward Crocus Hill Market,
    one desires to live. I wish there
    were wishes and not lists.
    I wish vegetables were grown
    by heart and artichokes would heal,
    I wish this rhythm
    of my approaching the butcher
    were more than a knuckle
    attaching itself to me
    perhaps a crocus, a
    root of limited possibilities,
    yet promising a livelihood.

42 AMARYLLIS

The orange metal plant spread its tendrils aloof over the museum's roof. With all its fragrant captivity asserting the immigrant rites of sculpture.

Restrained by metal from whispering, from complaint, even from homesickness, Amaryllis with its antique name, its distant origins, held a regal stance.

Between its position and the blockades of the city, between it and the nearest reliquary there would remain no communion. Amaryllis would never yield its superior stance. Its moods, glances, were those of an observer less restless as time passed, yet one who possessed the claim to restrict its grace.

There could be detected something of the borrower here, rather than the lender, an attitude the Museum's curator recognized would never change. He questioned the effect of those regal metal blooms upon the visitors. He worried if the city were aware of the undisturbed and selfish enchantment Amaryllis cast. A piece of art that through a collector's whim had come to dwell in Minneapolis.

LISSA MCLAUGHLIN

OO   O

IN CANADA

You try to live in Canada and where does it get you. Walking out of chimneys in the dead of winter you hook your feet tight to the branches of trees when the wind grabs you, the sky knuckles you on top of your head, bored as the rest of them. It wants to see you pick up and leave, so you bend your head back on itself and get fatter, twice as fat, watch out! Americans sneak over in boats, rifles in their boots, they push them inside their mouths just before they shoot. It's why you settle down in these spears, the tired Canadian cherry belching winter into its fruit. Indigestion's national, an old fury at the glee of this land. It's got so you don't know where to stand, straining from the ankles. Winter's thriving so well it's pushing you out of the tree, splitting the feathers on your breast, ramming your skin and sex as deep inside you as it can.

WIDOWS

Like walking through wet shirts the smell of the sea rides up your face in these coastal towns, you have to fight it off with a sleeve to breathe. The way people make pockets of their arms under avalanches.
Pouring up the street the smell bothers dogs. Clothes won't dry. Sometimes on top of a house a woman only tastes salt, she doesn't want to live.
Men knew how to build the little rooms, they could show plans. This model or that.

ANNA KARENINA

This Anna knows better. She doesn't want to see the news-paper's headline, "Wouldn't You Know She'd Screw Up?" scraping her face off the track. The train company cleaning up.

There must be another way around, so she gets a job in a factory. First she lops all her hair off within one inch of her famous stare. She's decided she'll invent snowshoes. Glue. Visor over her eyes, she works hard and makes the funds to buy out the factory. Every day sees her reissuing her spent self-image as self-improvement. She disappears from the factory one day, resumes her life as a dentist. She invents the artificial gum, then becomes a doctor and invents a pathetic but effective artificial waist. Roses are thrown to her in the street. She becomes a child psychiatrist and puts a wolf child on the road to civilization by convincing him his parents are really sheep. She recovers herself as many ways as she can think of. As a pornographer, followed for her ink-smudged lips. A vintner in North America, her incredible hair, grown back now, strung tight on its high winds. As an actress she knocks everyone dead. Forgiveness is in her fist. She possesses a waist so tiny women clutch themselves when they see it. Anna has fame now instead of notoriety, and can laugh. She chooses her lovers carefully, and afterwards shreds them like bad stocks. She even has her gender changed several times, and alters her hair color through a rainbow of violent hues.

But there is an unfortunate strain in Anna. One day she plunges into the ocean fully clothed. Seen by a whale, she is dragged back to the shore by the beast, to the applause of bathers. She survives falls, fires. Shot at dawn she is seen lifting like a lily above the rifles of the weeping firing squad, who fail to hear her swearing. She remains unmarked after taking into her bed men and women suffering from every disease. This only increases her lust.

At the root of it all, some real inability to adapt. Anna really only owned one act of resistance. Glancing up from her furs, she sometimes is forced to witness her own face, enormous and stupid as ever, coming at her like a train.

DAVID CHALONER

○   ○   ○

CHANGES

for Michael Palmer

heaviness transformed
an alert unfolding
she steps from the shadows
her name has changed
the strangeness of her ways
is nothing more than the strangeness
of her ways after all
personal details remain elusive
the scraps of paper that precede this
the notes leak from the aimless pen
the sky changes too
distorted by the temperate wind
and tarnished blades of sunlight
the day installs its memory
what you remember
may well happen

27 December 1972

LYN HEJINIAN

O   OO

NOTES TOWARD A LYRIC INTERLUDE

1   where awful love has closed upon my eye
the landscape of its armed embracing trees

he mentioned the silk and the sash

can read it   "purple"
              "pure"
              "partially"

you whom I've encountered all bloody
with love

2   that is a beautiful cat
and that is a beautiful child and
that is a beautiful color
and that is a beautiful view and
that is a beautiful tree
and, he said
that is a beautiful thought
and that is a beautiful poem and
that is a beautiful apricot
and that is a beautiful horse and
that is a beautiful day
and that is a beautiful melody and

3   villanelle
triolet
sestina
canzone

4 color of   (and lyrical)
   the declarative and the imperative
   "happier
   the elements are all here
   I recognize the thought and the dog
   "here
           the lion unleashed, the fucking lion
   a stone on the wall
   and
       shoorashing water

5 One wants to deny that others have felt what one now feels,
   have had the same or similar experiences. One wants to
   deny even their capacity for doing so. And, yet, one longs
   for their companionship, sympathy, and understanding. Per-
   haps, one wants to say, yes, you too have experienced this,
   but, of course, my experience means more to me than yours
   did to you — I am capable of feeling so much!

6 whisper
   wonder
   window
   plunder
   thunder

7 Tonight, he said, I am too tired
   it is too warm in here
   my bones are too tired
   and my eyes
   my bones and my eyes and my brain
   to write a love poem
   for you to write about love
   but not my heart
   to feel it

I'm willing to wake up because of the coffee
I'm willing to go out because of the new shoes
      and the sun
      the new shoes and the sun

     as
I'm willing to sleep
through all the nights of the earth
beside you

8 Think of it this way — if things of the moment are things
of the mind, then one lives in a synchronous universe.

9 Blinking waterfalls and sweet kisses!
   starlit leaf. The virtues of passion
   lay cool to the green, and cheeks
   (elbows, knees, breasts, etc.)
   beasts, a ritual
   and the truck in the field
   he repeated. The fruit on the ground
   between the red walls, the goats
   she sits, that lived in the country
   a laugh that's a pleasure
   but stars. I agree to be intimate
   of sorts, and round. It is wild of
   the ring
   the dance and splash the singing
   all his letters. I began
   fragments. — The smell then
   in their arrangement. The phrases of sound
   Blinking waterfalls and sweet kisses!

Such sweet - ness swells through these new days, - - -
In pure bird lat - in of his kind, - - -
Ab la dol - chor del temps no - vel - - -
Chan - tan chas-cus en lor la - ti - - -

The woods take leaf; each bird must raise
The mel - o - dy of a new song.
Foil - lo li bosc, e li au - cel
Se - gon lo vers del no - vel chan;

It's on - ly just a man should find
A - donc est - a ben c'om s'ai - si

His peace with what he's sought so long.
D'a - cho don hom a plus ta - lan.

GUILLAUME IX: NEW SONG FOR NEW DAYS

Such sweetness swells through these new days,
The woods take leaf; each bird must raise
In pure bird-latin of his kind,
The melody of a new song.
It's only just a man should find
His peace with what he's sought so long.

From her, where grace and beauty spring,
No message comes, no signet ring.
My heart can't rest and can't exult;
I don't dare move or take a stand
Until I know will peace result
And if she'll yield to my demands.

As for our love, you must know how
Love goes—it's like the hawthorn bough
That on the living tree stands, shaking
All night beneath the freezing rain
Till next day when the warm sun, waking,
Spreads through green leaves and boughs again.

That morning comes to mind once more
We two made peace in our long war;
She, in good grace, was moved to give
Her ring to me with true love's oaths.
God grant me only that I live
To get my hands beneath her clothes!

I can't stand their vernacular
Who keep my love from me afar.
By way of words, I guess I've found
A little saying that runs rife:
Let others mouth their loves around;
We've got the bread, we've got the knife.

MARCIA SOUTHWICK

o   o   o

ONCE, MY HUSBAND GAVE ME A HORSE

The barren women still roll
under the trees and do not sing . . .

I have sons who hang their clothes
in the trees

hoping the dead will slip
into the garments they recognize

and I say: you can break a few
of your belongings
to scatter over the graves, that's all.

You can give them these
and nothing more.

+

I spoke quietly,
I was not alone—

once, my husband gave me a horse;
he led it gently
through the faded grass.

I could hear one hoof
hit the gravel, then the second
and he said: Eskimos offer

fresh water to the seals,
oil to the birds,
arrows to the bears,

I will give you this horse
if you promise to ride away on it.

+

At the river, the children bathe
and turn away in the water.

The river is humming all around them;
their voices slide across the water.

On the bank, a lizard crawls out
from beneath a rock. It stares
and its body swells like a tiny black purse.

Even as it blinks, it stares
at the inside of its own eyelids.

+

I return to the town. The people
are building a house, and while I sleep

they measure my body. They place
the measurement under the stone.

They believe this will make
the building last forever.

Tomorrow, I will bury another stone
under the first. You can look all you like,

but this stone can burrow
almost as fast as a man can dig . . .

+

When the dead pass, the women do not sweep.
They cut locks of hair to lay in the road.
The children go to look for fire; they sing.

The dead come down to eat fish, ascending again
in the smoke of the fires they make—

and what they sing, no one can remember.

TOM AHERN

○   ○   ○

THE NEW LIFE

A *Letter in Passing to My Patrons*

A dog was kicked, so the report goes. Or slapped, as others tell it. And for this, two immense armies were gathered and this assembly slaughtered itself to some victory or another. And so nothing means anything particularly. As the report says.

Unimaginable patron, I beg you, is this what riches and fame amount to? Some would plot against you; there are rumors; but I shun them, and revile them in their hearing, nearly. Just between you and me, wealth *is* a curse. Dishonest fools think it's poverty. A true fool knows better.

But to rekindle the question. I'm plagued: And if imagination's a sham? What for poor scribblers then? My assets are liquid: they flow from my pen. Too liquid, some say; I hear these rumors. I grow garrulous. It's age.

A dog was kicked. Heavens descended and ascended. They fought like gods. Havoc, mayhem, suffering, despair. Was the dog saved? Famine, disease. And so forth. Was the dog scratching his fleas in all this?

Patron, unthinkable Patroness, I modestly submit to your eyes and their beyond-rumored graciousness these jottings. Pray smile on them, as they say you do occasionally. That in the mere existence of your virtue I may perhaps find my answer.

Introduction

Early in 1842 Nathaniel Hawthorne sketched in his notebook an idea for a tale.

"Some man of powerful character to command a person, morally subjected to him, to perform some act. The commanding person suddenly to die; and, for all the rest of his life, the subjected one continues to perform that act."

I will furnish this with a few necessary details — perhaps adapting Lord Chesterton's advice on dinner guests, that there be no fewer than the Graces and no more than the Muses.

But after some painful reflection I have decided to say nothing further concerning it.

Preface

. . . I part from my long though self-imposed task with some regret, in spite of the small toil it has cost and the very light sacrifices that such work, under present conditions, must involve. I am never likely to find either the patience, or the means, for another such. Even here I am troubled by the sense that there is more yet to be discovered about these few sketched lines . . .

Dedication

The fashion in dedications has altered so greatly over time that one scarcely knows how to start.

Should it be chapter or verse or a mere prepositional praise? And jostling me, entering by every door and window, were those who felt their names might rest easily here, as if this dull tongue were lodging for a night.

Yet behind this *mobile vulgus* (as the sour Dean would have swiftly branded them), I was glad to spy two old friends, whose patience, reserve, hospitality and kindness had often — more than often — astonished me. So to them — Sts. Anonimi Waldropinanitim — for lack of better payment and next month's rent, I dedicate these leaves and flowers.

I

"Oh," I added, quite seriously. "I do like kissing."

"Oh," she replied. Just an hour earlier she'd insisted I tell her whether I liked kissing or not. Now she was too distracted to care.

So begins my poor little story.

"That's not the way it happened at all!" she exclaimed. "The proper conduct of a love affair consists in registering accurately the electrical blips emitted by the lover."

"Oh," I mimicked her precisely. And began again my little tale, already a bit revised.

"But first . . ." she said.
"First?"
"A kiss."

II

I confess to you instantly and despite your opinion my taste for *comedie larmoyante*. It can't be stopped. I devour them whole, like the Orc, and swim back the next day for another look-see. It's probably much the same as my taste for a certain vanilla cookie, really a pastry rolled in sugar, and cut conventionally in the shapes of star, wing, leaf and doily. The same sort of excess *exactly*. I can eat them till my blood runs white. But since the centre of nature's everywhere, and boundaries nowhere, why worry? Everything's permissible, I suppose.

As for these *comedies*, you know what they are. Excuses to scourge women. *I* am not a scourger of women. I confess it; I apologize; I protest.

[*Tell here the story of Marina, an Indian secretary of Cortes.*]

You see we've gone a step from kissing. No need to guess where. It's a well-trod path, worn by innumerable heels. I'm not one of your coy authors, that ill-bred type who lead you by the nose to the bed, *then* insist you shut your eyes, plug your ears, and rely on memory or instinct or what-have-you. If you drop by, I'll give you the gruesome details.

Fortunately for the sake of my soul and whatever else is rattling around in my ribcage, I can ascribe all the blame — the first cause — to another. A powerful character, to whom I was morally subjected.

I modestly felt I might be a *little* imperfect in my perfection. He wanted *instead* to perfect this imperfection.

See what I mean? I'm sure you've noticed: there's always someone absolutely sweating to take your life in hand, pull you by the ear to some stranger's bed, tuck you in, and *instruct* you —the audacity!—in any number of outrages, of which variety is the least part.

I resisted. To eternity I resisted. But as I say, I was morally subjected. So in the end I consented.

III

Or pretended to.

"My butter-fiddle!" was how I usually began. He'd suggested "Sweetcakes!" — "Let hearts fly!" he'd argued. But I knew better. What fool would fall for such a sentiment. Too obvious, too saccharine. Too cruel.

And my successes won my case. If I were one to kiss-and-tell, oh the lips I could name! They pouted on some remarkable faces. Not that it ever went further than kissing. Or seldom. That was my method, see. Madness, eh? Hardly. I was just one to care for my health.

My "master" died soon after I'd started. And I mourned like a dog. Between meals. What I felt for him is best left unsaid, for the peace of his soul. The course he'd set was memorial enough. And I won't chase him to wherever he's gone with spite.

If I could just make a list . . . you'd see to what lengths my devotion had run! Tall, short, fat, slender, lovely or not, many degrees between. And these are simply physical matters. Intelligent, stupid; clever, dull. A variety of nice colors. I confess by the end my pretense was wearing a bit thin, poor cloak.

The end?

Well, I'm not writing from beyond the grave, though sometimes I wonder.

I changed masters is all. Nor unwillingly. And nor without the threat of death, if misery be counted.

IV

[*Tell here the story of how you met Ginger, La Pietra. How you fell in love against your own advice. How she was so much more cunning and intelligent. How you loved her till you thought you'd expire of it. How she tricked you. The conclusion.*]

Afterword

In a journal entry dated August 9th, 1842, Hawthorne wrote a few lines which serve:

"There is . . . an old stone pigsty, the open portion of which is overgrown with tall weeds, indicating that no grunter has recently occupied it . . . I have serious thoughts of inducting a new incumbent in this part of the parsonage. It is our duty to support a pig, even if we have no design of feasting upon him; and, for my own part, I have a great sympathy and interest for the whole race of porkers, and should have much amusement in studying the character of a pig. Perhaps I might try to bring out his moral and intellectual nature, and cultivate his affections."

Epilogue

Conventionally the epilogue mounts one of three burdens. But since one of those—a begging of the critics' and audience's indulgences—argues itself so fiercely in this instance, I fly to that and leave the others behind.

Mercy!! O Lord, mercy . . .

By the names of those that bore you, I didn't mean to, too.

Who takes bribes? Would you raise your hands please, so the ushers can find you. The claque needn't bother; you'll be getting a little something in the mail.

Recantation

Muhammed gave fair warning.

On the day of Judgment the Lord inspects every representation of a living thing. The angels then command the artisan to animate his creation. When he fails they'll cast him into Hell to the measure of his presumption. And believing this to be surely the case, before my God I go naked and hope this be burned before I take its place.

Translator's Note

I have tried within the limits of an English unfortunately splayed by Latinate and Germanic adhesions to render faithfully the original text. Its failures as a translation are of course my own. Much of the delicate versifying had to be conveyed in the rough carriage of prose; and certain idioms I regret are but distant cousins of those succinct proverbialisms so dear to its author. The substance and intention, however, are intact; and it is only the manner which has on occasion been abandoned.

DEBRA BRUCE

o   o   o

EPISTEMOLOGY

The foam of the apple
on your tongue
is the beginning:

You know
how your cells ingest,
sucking through their skins,
how the inner pods
store the life of the apple
in hot crystals.
Certain parts of you
repeat themselves;
The cell, in love with its image,
divides.
Ladders of mirrors
clutch their own rungs.
Certain parts
die hourly;
The outer gold of your wrist
scales off.
The lights of inner walls
drench themselves in darkness
each month.

You brush your hair in the mirror.
You feel the same.

That dancing like a moth
in your room. You know
it is you dancing.
Yours, the nightmare of horses
with manes draped like stone.
This page

BRUCE ANDREWS

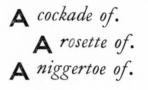

Contrary to metaphor staples fled from cardboard like a flock of psoriasis before the cure.

A *cockade of.*
A *rosette of.*
A *niggertoe of.*

The flower always
almond in person, baby.

Eggs embellish. **W**ords are your own
our own scooters.

Behind a shed of dirt skin seems whiter.

Is only the elastic.

I fall.

Both sexes.

The maneuvers of the **A**tlantic fleet.
nirvana = hit parade

Not any.　**S**trong
situation.

PHOSPHORUS

WALTER HALL

ooo

GLOWING IN THE DARK

There is no blue
in this blue flower.
The blue I see
is the rejected blue
that this blue flower won't absorb.

And a glance, at midnight,
at a luminescent clock
tells nothing.
The hands absorb the small put pure
light of the room

and the slow eye, focusing
after
the pale glow has soaked away,
misses the point   .
as the green hands blur

into time.
It is the failure of such things:
our dim machines,
composed of dissipating time and light
and just as frail,

ingest their intended possibilities
and soon reflect
only what might be left,
comprehension
chased into invisibility.

If I, in moments of inner darkness,
pass away
from light and my own matters, do I
reflect the life
I don't retain, as blue as this flower,

or is each life an isolated dawn
in space,
a light unframed by time, absorbed by
and reflecting purely
every color, whole, within its wave?

OCTOBER

Winter cannot sleep. It tosses
its windy head and barks. Everyone
is coming back. Those people
you thought you'd insulted finally
and forever are beating their smiles
against your glass door, as perennial
as allergies. But look at yourself
in the same glass. How can
your eyes droop so low
with your face hanging out that far?
Be objective. Forget your miseries.
Consider nebulae. Why, your perceptions
are so slow that when you think
you see a star explode, you don't.
It happened long ago. But look.
Things are going more our way than ever.
No traffic tickets now for quite a while
(no car), there's an art museum
within a hundred miles, your cheeks
are filling out, your library is the best
it's ever been. Who knows.
It might even rain enough this year.
So whoever wants to get up or out
or in or through, let them.
As they open their mouths
to excuse themselves, imagine rocks
inching down the eroded hills.
The best you can do is watch it happen.

RUTH KRAUSS

O   OO

From WHEN I WALK I CHANGE THE EARTH

I — the speaker — walk and
Grass begins Flowers Trees Birds Bees Animals Stones move
Houses appear Lightning Thunder and Downpour
Water grows Waves Expanses as far as can be seen
Rocking grows
a Chair and is sat on
an Apple and is eaten disappears ah poor if personified one!
a Platitude comes — take your own — wearing a dunce cap
and walking down a street bowing then dances and is joined
by a Multitude of more-and-other-Platitude they dance
    together
I — the Speaker — also dance
play a Piano banging away at the Keys that are flying
hitting Windows and Doors and breaking them
Now a Wet Dream comes drying in a Wind
the Sky breaks open in a loud Sun Shine and is followed
by Him or Her I sing loud and bad howling I
fly out of my skin and more naked and dancing more lala
carrying a Piano and crushed under it I
am followed then by a Troup of Sorrows in a cortege ending
at the Hospital full of many repeats of I Self Me Him or
Her It sitting standing in bed filling out forms
Pest and sure looks it!
Cans of Stuff shake out of the air and over the Pests
I hang symbolic impalata the Scene grows more
tropic Explosions People flying out all over
creeps in Corruption and pulls switch to a
Green Dawn if not personified green grows the air
the Earth shakes and opens and falls we hear It
our Future appears on wings

133

Orange the color turns gray that was blue
and a curious Light over All
potatoes potatoes potatoes
Narcissus falls into Water and is not beautiful only drowned
he-she goes up in steam along with Hyacinthus Leda and
the swan of Jesus
as is stated
a literal stoning of I Everyone from Everywhere
Desolation — looks like What — comes out on a leash turns
returns leaps the land of China leaps
the Moon and a pair of Shoes leap
Holding-One-Another is Everywhere a God goes backward
laughing or is it crying going on
no sooner said than done
Leaves enter and surround the trees with green making the air
more blue I roll in like a tumbler in somersaults I
lie down and look up the Sun is shining my eyes are
closing eyes are closed and the Sun
can no longer be for me Night comes on and takes over and
   we
do not know what is happening

LARRY EIGNER

O   O   O

From LINED   *UP*   *BULK*   *SENSES*

we are playing
a game   paradise

a cliff

a sort of blue

shading out

of

the fences now

indeterminacy of love
you   there

on looking back

gradations of the sky
variety

continuous heavens it
blends with fields

music
of a surface
brought in

as orbits

indiscriminate, indeterm-
inate, we
should have all the time

ourselves

at last

you go far

Listening to the sea
without a shell

a shell

rises and falls in the air

the mind

KENWARD ELMSLIE

o   oo

COMMUNICATIONS EQUIPMENT

Fall output hotbed.
Sorted out algebraic mosaic
buckles from skywave, wrap it up!
Sun up in sky frontal straight
veers off into coyote yowl
issuing forth from human throat.
Go-between wizardry, thrill of.

Over to picaresque puttering,
cut off from channel of dubbed-in choice.
Cut-off point is what I do,
down to amuse through trapdoor,
flea circus in muffin (interior buzz)
to which add chortles at the portholes,
glutted bubble-dancers glaring out,
lip-read answers wearing thin,
fol-de-rol about mutt bumblebees
zonked on cold mums,
bone orchard mums cat's night out.

Kinky gentry into ransom crud used up.
Holding our own in flustery weather used up.
Many restful oases here in Hat City,
same old snappy salutes at the roadblocks
where om-like hum of shoot-out traffic
of scant interest to us fine-eared hold-outs,
honed to love outcries in the painted desert,
shrieks from humanoid wind tunnels.

Youth blur memory descends the staircase
now hidden by rock formations
and out the door.

Undervalue love object, fear of death rattle.
Overvalue love object, fear of breath battle.

Strobe allows scant time to dredge deep —
microscopic attention span units
run for cover like clobbered roadrunners
seeing bio-feedback chameleons in the sky,
hammers and fireworks pulsating,
tickertape huzzahs.

Hula biz for rent,
mood music booed.
What first President underwater reef,
riding in an auto to Mobile offshore.

Moth-eaten defeats bombard the senses.
Totaled hotbox.
Who said hot wax?

Tiptoe through the hydrants
out to where orange dabs
(shy dance) carouse down
like silly symphony moths,
strident franchises
of dried A to Z embryos.

Here comes the goof
looking for proof,
he of the baffling accident pile-up,
airline an almost not there line,
bolero about defective sky forests,
leafless but rare.
We never close,
radio low,
flash flood.

CALVIN FORBES

o   o   o

DEBATING WITH J. C.

Shine met Jesus at the well
And said how do you do!
I'm alright sinner, how about you?
You ready for hell?

No, Shine said. That water's
Too bitter, don't suit
My taste. Life is rough enough.
Why go down yonder?

Lord, please grant me a parole?
Nay, Shine. You been unhappy anyway.
Why stay another day?
Plus you too old

For lust, too young for love.
Shine confessed his time
Was spent drinking and gambling.
So God sent a dove.

But Shine wanted a crow.
It's good to know Shine won
The debate without a knife or a gun.
My shadow won't grow;

It's the cross I bear.
Forty days without any women
Was an omen. Now
My vision is clear as desert air.

TRAVELING IS SO ENLIGHTENING

The Golden Gate Bridge reminds Shine
Of the wire he had in his mouth as a child.
Gums forlorn, bow-legged teeth,
And braces until he was twenty-one.

Shine travels through Nebraska
The land as flat as his nose,
One ocean behind him like a squaw.
Upsouth singing a song as he meditates:

If you never wash your neck
And dirt collects
Thick as a second skin,
Then you don't have to worry.
You won't get a red neck.

Shine drives a limousine.
A man's car, Shine whispers,
Should be as comfortable as his livingroom.
Smoking a reefer thick as his thumb,

He flicks his ashes
In every state and arrives
In New Orleans looking for a new Dream Book.
But he returns to Harlem in one piece.

Shine where you been —
Back and around the world again.
I've seen things that best remain unsaid.
One sure thing I learnt: Kiss
ASS and you shall receive.

SUSAN HANKLA

RUNNING HOME

I am running home again,
past the trees by the trailers and up Tank Hill.

I am running home.
After the snares of school, after the oiled floors
that smudged my socks, after the ache of being taught,

I am running home.

I am running past the cemetery
and the legless man at the A&P,
and the liquor store women in fake furs,
and the cowboys in English Leather aftershave
who sit on the corner.
I am running past the pervert with the monkey on his
    shoulder,
who stuck by me through all those Saturdays.

I run past the florist shop,
where I bought three velvet roses,
and Mrs. Wilson's yard, where she circles the house
and checks the locked windows for broken locks.
Her head turns as I fly past.

I run with an aching bladder.
I am almost in tears.
I am swimming under water. I am writing summer letters
out under the awning. I am fixing up a tea party
to serve my lost friends. We will comment on the apples
rotting on the trees. We will dance in the sudden hail
under the rising moon.

I am running to that room
with its walls of night and its ceiling of stars,
where I dreamed who I'd be,
praying the house would be safe from fire.

I am running home to 306 Grayson
with its brass door knocker
that remembers my name,
but no one listens to my frantic knocking
and I hear a vacuum cleaner from the tunnels deep inside
growing louder and louder in this final refrain.

I turn around sadly, my shadow crossing the door,
and that tall repeating mirror
watches me from its perch upstairs,
and looks out from the house of who I was,
and loses me as I walk away, slowing down, collecting myself,
and sees me disappear,
and lets me out of its sight, at last,
at last so I can write:
"I am running home."

DAVID MILLER

o   o   o

PRIMAVERA

1 that I loved them, & that meant
loving them forever a small window
that for me it would be an *eternal*
memory
lost a darkness utterly black
travel no visible record

2 so this is *image* poetry? he asked
no I said the voices faded in
afternoon air noise of traffic
early heat
I walked with my back to him
away into the crowd then turned
to face him he had already stopped filming

3 white chalk on a blackboard
blue chalk on a blackboard
green chalk on a blackboard
yellow chalk on a blackboard
white blue green yellow
chalk on the pavement

4 those children will take your hand
because unable to tell you
lead you away
they may kiss your mouth
to stop your commands
they will avoid your eyes then perhaps
stare fixedly into them
& then not look at your eyes again

5   light changing the features
    right side of the face
    I mean, scarcely visible in reproduction

6   the telephone the small window
    table
    no words
    a gap at the heart of things
    black space exactly next to
    the light from the window

7   "looking into" someone's face
    then hearing their words over the telephone
    table centre of the room
    diffused light of the afternoon

8   walking in the woods for miles
    then coming into my room
    beyond allegory beyond dreams
    pavement the only guide
    the figure stopped put her head to the window
    looking out
    her eyes pensive

9   two figures (one my friend) their backs
    both of them facing
    that wall
    the Wailing Wall
    a death

10 a wood a forest my own youth
    city material images of high contrast
    footsteps through a doorway to follow the differences
    in how we walked
    between some fragments O light of spring

GEORGE TYSH

○   ○   ○

TEA

It is one of my favorite things.
A severe mind loses its head.
To bring you a book whose pages are
points in a line: one two three four etc.

A HOLE

I begin the performance
light-headed from grains.
The ego is nothing but a mushroom
which disappears after death.
Death is represented by two wobbly lines.
The poetry of this thought splashes
cold water inside my head
and saves a minute more from sleep.
Where are you now. I can't help
thinking. Reflection works.
I keep going back into it
in time of trouble. The minute
has become five. The music in
my head goes on, over and over
and becomes a hole.

THE END

moustache: intellect
zipper: blossoms
sex: my only weakness
mind: won't work
my story's been told

WILLIAM DORESKI

ꝏ

UNION SQUARE

The moon spreads lies: wedding ring, cunt. The Somerville Werewolves
Steal a car on Highland Street, their bodies packed in vaseline . . .
If I could kill for a meal I'd do it. Moon in the junkyard;
Exploded views of automobiles; here I could rust for the sake of love
And no one need pity Thin Man and his pockets full of postcards.
Now the stolen car whines downhill to Union Square, corner kids wave,
Their paws glisten in the streetlights. One night they'll shred me in passing.
As I run, trailing tails of flesh like streams of moonlight in the woods,
Their laughter will dismiss all this foreplay with the dark.

EAST SOMERVILLE

Streets named after states. The convent destroyed by a mob. I smell fire:
Plenty of aged warehouses ripe for the adolescent's torch.
Sunburnt, drooly for beer, I feel the crowd gather me. We're all friends:
Even the gangsters smile too much because they live on an island.
If I floated overland to count the three-decker rooftops
I could embrace the town for a laugh. Monotonous? Only one life
To spend — I've travelled in Somerville as Thoreau in Concord, among men
Rather than through the clay-pit ponds where disgusting gods have stepped.
And here the day-old bread goes sweet as the body of a saint.
The sweat of the dumb is pure beer, I'll gladly lick a foot or two
To prove good Catholics can share. These streets remember their war dead
The way a dog remembers his name. And you? I've learned to wear the
  crowd
Of retired Irish cops and truck drivers and mailmen
The way a lion wears his mane — with a roaring indolence
And a conviction that the kill will come to meet me if I'm calm
And save my claws for thrills in private.

FOUR A.M., UNION SQUARE

Dead hour, not a dog's bark. No stones afoot. Time to swallow
The graveyard stories and cry. I'm bodily still, and graceless,
But I fear only the small things: rods and scalpels and tortured meat.
Jesus Saves, but here the wind breaks over tenements where arsonists
Test children in the tortures of sleep. So much discussion of bombs
While the whole snoring world goes off like a fart in the President's bath.
No one's listening: I'll spit in the public fear, the silence
Turns in the bed of the river, and lifts one spaniel ear.

RUSSELL EDSON

o   o   o

THE EVENING MEAL

A mouse watched from the dark of its place. It was getting on to dinner time, so the mouse calculated by the rising tide of its hunger, stimulated, no doubt, by the sounds in the kitchen, as Mrs. George beat an ox to death with her apron strings, enticing it with the very apron like a matador.

The mouse heard the ox pleading with Mrs. George, please, Mrs. George, that hurts.

The mouse heard the flapping of vultures landing on the roof.

Mr. George was on the telephone making an appointment for a hearse to remove the dinner scraps.

The ox was stampeding in the kitchen.

Mr. George shouted, can you hold it down, honey? I'm on the phone.

Everything normal: four o'clock, the dinner ox being killed, Mr. George on the telephone ordering a hearse, the ox pleading with Mrs. George, the ox stampeding and Mr. George asking Mrs. George to quiet the ox while he ordered the hearse . . .

But then Mr. George's son began to annoy Mr. George.

Stop annoying me, said Mr. George.

I want to annoy you, said his son.

Stop annoying me, screamed Mr. George.

And then Mr. George was asking his wife for her apron strings . . .

At last Mrs. George was dragging the dead ox into the dining room by its back legs.

Mr. George pointed to their son on the floor, he annoyed me.

Apron strings are probably the cruelest of weapons, thinks the mouse in the dark of its place; surely this will delay dinner . . .

JOHN ENGMAN

○   ○○

ALCATRAZ

I can't recall the name of the old cafe
but I saw the famous San Francisco dream there
and people sipping chocolate while gazing at a blue bay.
A local woman made advances with a few remarks
about the deep, subconscious sea. I watched the gulls
circle tables, then I told them to go away.

I tried to put down on paper what made me
feel a certain way. I said rain was long black hair
in oceanic waves. But the sun was shining, as I remember,
and a blonde woman at the next table was memorable.
We talked until we found we held something in common,
both of us were Minnesotans and so we laughed until

we screamed. For a dime in the Automatic-Eye
I saw all I really cared to see of Alcatraz:
a man with a spyglass looking back at me. Gulls flew
across his polyester shirt, I could see him that clearly.
He must have watched me drinking my *cafe au lait!*
I saluted him across the bay. He raised an eyebrow.
Then a fatter woman ran at him with an Instamatic. *Edna!*
he must have said, *Come quick! People are waving.*

WISHING

for George

Here we are parked in the photograph of a Pontiac
with wheels made of snow. The snow has stopped
against the wheels like a flight of dead moths.
This is our winter migration, we have to walk.
You are in red, I in my old blue winter coat.
This is another storm in Minnesota, 1964.
We are going nowhere dressed so warm.
We are lost, as children tend to be, near home.

While we sat on the hood of this old sedan
our fathers shoveled and spoke about the end
a certain mystery could come to if we touched it
gently with our hands. This mystery
escaped the 8x5. It was the hammer of shovels
on hubcaps and the frozen road, our fathers'
breathing like a sound we'd never heard before
from nails driven into hard, wet wood.

As always the mystery is ruined by a photograph.
Photography is silence. Everyone knows that.
Photography is what we do to wish for too much.
Wishing is what our fathers did. We wish
we'd saved the photographs that show how
evolution fills the gaps: Pontiacs, our fathers
on the brink of happiness. Minnesota, 1964. Another
storm. We disappeared although we only meant to blink.

HARRISON FISHER

o   o   o

ON THE PEDESTRIAN

As the first child
destroys the illusion of imparted perfection,
the second is even a greater step
toward despair.

Nothing can be
duplicated right;
the dream child
saves himself for his spaces,
lives in the spaces between his parts.

A stray mole for an elbow
(the black sun of the only heaven's sky)
or throat (the pulse of great waters), a red
birthmark (by this and to this, the struggle)
a crescent — these conspire

their imprinting on flesh,
markers for a person
like blank instructions for the turning of centuries,

the third child who outlives them all, yet is ugly
and is himself the news of the evening sun,
the cul-de-sac.

THE TARGET BEING

Something large claims I am a part of it. I insist on my own autonomy and tell it to get lost. Soon, it is lost.

Then I meet you. I become a fool for your attention, saying anything to keep you listening, looking at me.

The announcement of everything about myself takes only a few days. I sit before you like a residue, thinking I have burned every secret I own and what will I do now?

Then I realize it displeases you that I am not part of some larger thing. We have both watched me exterminate my past in a matter of sentences. The future is mouthed just as easily when I talk of what I will do.

In truth, I will do nothing.

That vastness that pulls all forward together takes you. You go forward. I insist on myself, this cabal of particles that have coalesced from nowhere, too dulled by their love for each other to separate, to take the air for a chance to survive.

EVERYTHING'S DERBY

And when I dream of lostness,
I come to a beach to find myself
headless gulls beating the air.
I promise to give them
heads in my next dream; for now, I say,
you gulls are as beautiful, even though
stumped, as butterflies. Next time
you may use your heads to read
my poems. Do you like poems?
Then my darkest night comes.
I sleep with zinnias.
They brighten the bed.
I dream Zero.

HARRY MATHEWS

oo   o

TRADITION AND THE INDIVIDUAL TALENT:
THE "BRATISLAVA SPICCATO"

In August 1877 the celebrated conductor Jeno Szenkar, who six weeks earlier had gone to Graz to visit his friend the violinist Benno Bennewitz, and incidentally to perform with him the cycle of the Beethoven violin sonatas, left that city for Budapest, where he was engaged to conduct two operas at the summer festival. This was the Jeno Szenkar whose wife's elder brother was the grandfather of Geza Anda. Benno Bennewitz for his part was Teresa Stich-Randall's maternal great-grandfather, and his niece was Dietrich Fischer-Dieskau's mother. Szenkar's stay in Graz had been motivated not by professional reasons but by concern for his health. The winter in Vienna had become a grueling one, since he not only had been chief conductor at the Staatsoper but had prepared several concerts with the Philharmonic Orchestra: it was in connection with the latter responsibility that he had become involved in bitter public controversy with Ludwig Krumpholz (who, much later, was Hermann Scherchen's godfather) over the performance of the cadenzas in Joseph-Leopold Pitsch's posthumous piano concerto. Pitsch's widow, the following year, was to marry Karl Knappertsbusch and by him bear the father of Hans Knappertsbusch. The unexpected battle with Krumpholz had lessened the benefits brought him by the assistance of young Franz Mittag. (Mittag as an infant had shared a wetnurse with Irmgaard Dehn, for whom her granddaughter Irmgaard Seefried was named.) This was no fault of Mittag: he had done brilliant work, and thanks to the impression he then made he was named only two years later to the directorship of the opera, after a year's interim under the aging Julius Meyer-Remy, the great-grandfather of both Hugo Meyer-Welfing and Mrs. Rudolph Bing. Szenkar had finished the season in a state of exhaustion, and he had dearly counted on his sojourn in Graz to restore him.

The concerts with Bennewitz required little exertion — playing the piano was for him a pastime, he loved his fiddler friend, it was the best kind of busman's holiday. His hopes of recovery, however, were disappointed, for he had hardly been in Budapest a week when he died, felled by a stroke during a rehearsal of *Childe Harold*. This now-forgotten opera was by Bela Hubay, whose great-grandson married George Szell's sister.

Szenkar was much loved in Budapest, and although he was taken for burial to his home town of Kaposvar, the city put on a grand memorial service for him. To this event many musicians came from all over Central Europe.

Among them was the Czech violinst Vaclav Czegka. The Czegkas have of course always been a central force in the musical life of their country — Rafael Kubelik is Vaclav Czegka's great-great-nephew. A lifelong friend of Szenkar, of whom he was a little the senior, Czegka undertook the trip to Budapest without hesitation, but not without misgiving, for his own health was frail. Accordingly he sent a telegram to his son Frantisek (who would three years later marry Clara Riemen-schneider, the grandmother of Inge Borkh), a musician himself, then touring in Klagenfurt: he should journey at once to Gyor, where he would join his father, who would thus not have to travel alone all the way from Brno to Budapest. It should perhaps be mentioned that Czegka had lived by himself since the death of his wife the year before. She had been born a Kalli-woda, a family to which Rudolph Firkusny is related.

During the train ride a certain line of thought that Czegka had been following for many months at last reached its conclusion. It had started at the very performance by Krumpholz of the Pitsch concerto that had given Szenkar such trouble. Through an adroit combination of pedaling and touch Krumpholz had demonstrated a novel effect, that of making the hammers "bounce drily" on the strings. Czegka had then begun wondering whether the violin bow could not produce a similar effect. He had pondered, he had experimented, above all he had discussed the matter daily with his son-in-law, the cellist Jan Sevcik. (Through her remarriage with Laszlo Thoman, Sevcik's mother would have a grandson who was second cousin once removed of Ferenc Fricsay and first cousin twice removed of Sandor Vegh.) Before their discussions could bear fruit, Sevcik had left for Ljubljana, where he was engaged to play with Gustav Henschkel (Clemens Krauss's maternal grandfather) and Friedrich Rheinberger. It was on this occasion that Rheinberger met Olga Czerny (no relation), whom he later married and by whom he had several children, none of them musical. Rheinberger's sister, however, was Wolfgang Windgassen's grandmother, and one of his brothers was throughout their school years the best friend of Wolfgang Schneiderhan's father.

It was as his train pulled into the Bratislava station that Vaclav Czegka discovered how the desired "dry bounce" could be realized. Such was his astonishment that he cried out, and under the strain of that cry he felt his old heart falter. He looked around for a confidant to whom, in case the worst happened, he might entrust his secret. No one besides a very old lady shared his compartment. He strode the length of his car but only traveling salesmen, governesses with children, and other hopeless cases were to be seen. Unwisely he leaped from the train onto the station platform, and doing so felt a surge of darkness within him. The platform was empty except for a young rabbi. Czegka staggered toward him, fell on his knees, and managed to gasp out his discovery before his heart quite collapsed.

The rabbi, who had, although he was Russian, a good grasp of German, was Nathan Milstein's father. Returning to Odessa, he repeated what he had learned to a professor at the St. Petersburg Conservatory, Boris Zaremba. (He was the great-uncle both of Boris Khaikin and, through a niece's Bulgarian marriage, Boris Christoff.)

These facts supply a partial explanation of the excellence of Russian violinists in the twentieth century, and clarify the origins of the controversial expression "Bratislava spiccato."

HEATHER S. J. STELIGA

○ ♂

POEM ON MY BIRTHDAY

1   I have lost everything.
    What I have not lost, I've wasted.
    And yet your rowing takes me nowhere.

2   I find a net
    and throw it around the objects that attacked you.
    I see only objects.

3   Where did that dark boat go?

MALIBU

Our palomino is a champion sprinter
through these waters

We are nearing the thin wind
in the cedar trees

There the gold Moebius strip
fits our fingers

GENTLE ONE

So now
I am your little lamb.

You will pray for me.

You will slap me hard
across the face
when I say Let me die.

You will hold me,
give me water.

You will kick me
to the island.

CROSSROADS

1 We see men
pissing
by the side of the road.
You draw
Mesopotamia.
I draw
a buffalo.

2 There are your fingers but
there are those cactus places
behind your shirt.
I
unbutton
your collar.
Soon I will tear off your shirt.
I will see your heart is a tattoo.
I don't want to look.

3 Everything rises.
Blood tongues
rise.
Flowers rise.
I dive
and I rise.

4 The museum curator
wears ashes in his pants.
We eat blueberry muffins
all through the museum.
We laugh at the same paintings &
drink coffee.

5 Angels of perfection & goddesses of beauty!

6 The snow is so deep.
We say October October &
California.
We roll bolts of thread
to the coast.

ROSMARIE WALDROP

O   OO

THE SENSES BRIEFLY: A LETTER

".... it is annoying to tell you
how
the picture you took
of laughter in the window
shows
that you perfect what you try to
escape because
in between these lips there's
something"
     which blows
     which blows

but inexorably
you don't see the error the quiet arrival
because the piano leaves you indifferent

a word
in the eyes of
insatiable
    can't you find her ubiquitous body?

as if in an unknown
identity
mad and tonedeaf
she expects fat letters

but somehow forgets
     the indigo
     divan

and wednesday had this
this voice which waits for
the horn
the repetition
    the excitement

bibliography ∘∘∘

BOOKS & BOOKLETS

1. **D. C. Hope** (ed.), *The Wolgamot Interstice* (an anthology of poems by Donald Hall, X. J. Kennedy, Dallas Wiebe, James Camp, John Heath-Stubbs, Bernard Keith, D. C. Hope, W. D. Snodgrass, with an introduction by Bernard Waldrop, projector for the John Barton Wolgamot Society). 51 pp. Designed, linotyped and printed letterpress by Joe Gula. 9x6, saddlestitched. 1000 copies. Ann Arbor & Detroit, 1961.

2. **Keith Waldrop** (translator), *Federico Garcia Lorca: Poem of the Gypsy Seguidilla.* 20 pp. printed on recto. Handset in 12 pt. Caslon Oldstyle and printed letterpress by Keith Waldrop in "a small edition for friends." Cover and title page have woodcuts by Keith Waldrop. 10½x7¼, saddlestitched. Durham, CT, 1967.

3. **Rosmarie Waldrop**, *A Dark Octave* (poems). 24 pp. printed on recto. Handset in 12 pt. Caslon Oldstyle and printed letterpress on Parchment Deed by Keith Waldrop. The 2-color title page has a linoleum cut by Keith Waldrop. 8x5¾, saddlestitched. 100 numbered copies. Durham, CT, 1967.

4. **James Camp**, *The Gnostic World View* (poem). 6 pp. printed on recto. Handset in 12 & 24 pt. Caslon Oldstyle with an ornamental initial and printed letterpress by Keith Waldrop. 11x7½, saddlestitched. 35 numbered copies, all signed on the Japanese rice paper cover. Scheidt Head Press & Burning Deck, Durham, CT, 1968.

5. **Alan Sondheim**, *an, ode* (poems). 40 pp. Offset from typewriter. Cover by Keith Long. 11x8½, saddlestitched. 700 copies. Providence, 1968.

6. **Alan Sondheim**, *Sequences* (visual poem). 8 pp. 36 pt. Futura Demi, offset on Tweedweave. Designed by the author. 11x8½, sidestitched. Providence, 1968.

7. **Keith & Rosmarie Waldrop**, *Change of Address* (poem in collaboration). 8 pp. handset in 12 pt. Caslon Oldstyle and printed letterpress in "a small edition for friends" by Rosmarie Waldrop. Cover photo by Walt Odets. 7½x11, saddlestitched. Providence, 1968.

8. **James Camp**, *An Edict From the Emperor* (poems). 32 pp. printed on recto. Handset in 12 pt. Caslon Oldstyle and printed letterpress by Rosmarie Waldrop. Cover photo by Keith Waldrop. 10x7 saddlestitched. 225 numbered copies. Providence, 1969.

9. **Anneliese Ott**, *Offene Sekunde* (poems in German). 24 pp. printed on recto. Handset in 12 pt. Caslon Oldstyle and printed letterpress. by Rosmarie Waldrop. Woodcut on cover by Keith Waldrop. 9x7, saddlestitched. 100 numbered copies. Providence, 1969.

10. **Dorothy Donnelly**, *Houses* (poems). 24 pp. printed on recto. Handset in 12 pt. Caslon Oldstyle and printed letterpress in 2 colors by Keith Waldrop. 9½x6½, saddlestitched, in Tweedweave wrappers. 150 numbered copies. Providence, 1970.

11. **John Heath-Stubbs**, *Artorius, Book I* (poem). 40 pp. Handwritten and designed by Keith Waldrop. Offset. 8½x5½, saddlestiched. 250 copies. Providence, 1970.

12. **Peyton Houston,** *For the Remarkable Animals* (poems). 20 pp. printed on recto. Handset in 12 pt. Caslon Oldstyle and printed letterpress on Curtis Rag by Rosmarie Waldrop. 10x7, saddlestitched, in Tweedweave wrappers. 150 numbered copies. Providence, 1970.

13. **X. J. Kennedy,** *Bulsh* (poems). 68 pp. printed on recto. Handset in 18 pt. Caslon Oldstyle & 48 pt. Cable Extra Bold and printed letterpress by Keith Waldrop. 5x7, saddlestitched, in wrappers. 110 numbered, signed copies. Providence, 1970.

14. **Christopher Middleton,** *The Fossil Fish* (15 micropoems). 36 pp. printed on recto. Handset in 12 pt. Caslon Oldstyle and printed letterpress on Curtis Rag by Rosmarie Waldrop. 2 colors throughout. Cover by Keith Waldrop. 10x6, saddlestitched, in Tweedweave wrappers. 150 numbered copies. Providence, 1970.

15. **Carl Morse,** *Dive* (poems). 36 pp. printed on recto. Handset in 12 pt. Caslon Oldstyle and printed letterpress on Curtis Rag by Rosmarie Waldrop. 2 colors throughout. Cover by Keith Waldrop. 10x7, saddlestitched, in Tweedweave wrappers. 150 numbered copies. Providence, 1970.

16. **Terry Stokes,** *The Night Ed Sullivan Slapped One of the Kessler Twins Right on the Ass in the Middle of His Show & Their Song & Dance* (poem). 20 pp. printed on recto. Handset in 12 pt. Caslon Oldstyle & 24 pt. Bernhard Gothic Bold and printed letterpress on Curtis Rag by Rosmarie Waldrop. 2 colors throughout. 6x10, saddlestitched, in Tweedweave wrappers. 100 numbered copies. Providence, 1970.

17. **Keith Waldrop,** *The Antichrist* (poems). 34 pp. printed on recto. Handset in 12 pt. Caslon Oldstyle and printed letterpress by Rosmarie Waldrop. Cover photo by George Manupelli. 9½x7½, saddlestitched. 150 numbered copies. Providence, 1970.

18. **Keith & Rosmarie Waldrop,** *Letters* (concrete poems). 36 pp. printed on recto. Various typefaces and colors. Letterpress on Linweave Text. Printed by the authors. 7¼x10, saddlestitched, in Tweedweave wrappers. 500 numbered copies. Providence, 1970.

19. **Rosmarie Waldrop,** *Camp Printing* (visual poems). 40 pp. printed on recto. Offset from letterpress and collage transformations of poems by James Camp. 9½x11, sidestitched. 500 copies. Providence, 1970.

20. **Rosmarie Waldrop,** *The Relaxed Abalone* (poems). 32 pp. printed on recto. Handset in 18 pt. Caslon Oldstyle and printed letterpress by Keith Waldrop, with a 2-color titlepage. 9½x5, saddlestitched. 150 numbered copies. Providence, 1970.

21. **George Tysh,** *Mecanorgane* (poems). 44 pp. printed on recto. Handset in 12 pt. Caslon Oldstyle and printed letterpress by Rosmarie Waldrop. 9½x6¼, saddlestitched, in Tweedweave wrappers. 250 numbered copies. Providence, 1971.

22. **Keith Waldrop,** *My Notebook for December* (poems). 26 pp. Handset in 12 pt. Caslon Oldstyle and printed letterpress on Curtis Rag by Rosmarie Waldrop. 2 colors throughout. 7x7, saddlestitched, in Tweedweave wrappers. 400 numbered copies. Providence, 1971.

23. **Tom Ahern,** *The Transcript* (a story). 28 pp. Offset from typewriter, 3-color letterpress cover by Rosmarie Waldrop. 8½x7, saddlestitched. 500 copies. Providence, 1972.

24. **Mary Ashley,** *Truck (A Dance)* (poem and dance program). 60 pp. Offset and letterpress on Linweave Text. Design by Keith Waldrop. 7x7 (text pages 4¼x7), saddlestitched, in Tweedweave wrappers. 200 copies. Providence, 1972.

25. **William Bronk,** *Utterances* (3 poems). 12 pp. printed on recto. Handset in 18 & 24 pt. Caslon Oldstyle and printed letterpress on Warren Antique by Keith Waldrop. 2 colors throughout. 11x8½, saddlestitched, in Tweedweave wrappers. 250 numbered copies. Providence, 1972.

26. **Ray DiPalma,** *All Bowed Down* (poems). 20 pp. printed on recto. Handset in 12 pt. Caslon Oldstyle and printed letterpress, with a 2-color titlepage, by Rosmarie Waldrop. 9½x6¼, saddlestitched, in Tweedweave wrappers. 250 numbered copies. Providence, 1972.

27. **Walter Hall,** *Glowing in the Dark* (poems). 40 pp. printed on recto. Handset in 12 pt. Caslon Oldstyle and printed letterpress by Rosmarie Waldrop. 9½x6¼, saddlestitched, in Tweedweave wrappers. 250 numbered copies. Providence, 1972.

28. **Christopher Middleton,** *Briefcase History* (poems). 40 pp. printed on recto. Handset in 12 Caslon Oldstyle and printed letterpress by Rosmarie Waldrop. 9½x6¼, saddlestitched, in Tweedweave wrappers. 250 numbered copies. Providence, 1972.

29. **Tom Ryan,** *Encephalogeorgics* (poems). 26 pp. printed on recto. Handset in 12 pt. Caslon Oldstyle and printed letterpress by Rosmarie Waldrop. 2 colors throughout. 8x5, saddlestitched, in Tweedweave wrappers. 250 numbered copies. Providence, 1972.

30. **Kirk Wilson,** *The Early Word* (6 poems). 20 pp. printed on recto. Handset in 12 pt. Caslon Oldstyle and printed letterpress by Rosmarie Waldrop. 2 colors throughout. 9½x6¼, saddlestitched, in Tweedweave wrappers. 250 numbered copies. Providence, 1972.

31. **Bruce Andrews,** *Corona* (poems). 30 pp. Handset in 12 pt. Caslon Oldstyle and printed letterpress on Warren Antique by Rosmarie Waldrop. 2 colors throughout. 4¾x6¼, saddlestitched, in Tweedweave wrappers. 300 numbered copies. Providence, 1973.

32. **Judith Grossman,** *Frieze* (a story). 20 pp. Offset. Letterpress title page & cover by Keith Waldrop. 8½x7, saddlestitched, in Cortlea cover. 250 copies. Providence, 1973.

33. **Rochelle Owens,** *Poems from Joe's Garage.* 20 pp. Handset in 12 & 24 pt. Caslon Oldstyle and printed letterpress on Warren Antique by Rosmarie Waldrop. 2 colors throughout. 12½x8, saddlestitched, in Tweedweave wrappers. 250 numbered copies. Providence, 1973.

34. **Peter Riley,** *Strange Family* (12 songs). 26 pp. Handset in 12 pt. Caslon Oldstyle and printed letterpress on Warren Antique by Rosmarie Waldrop. 2 colors throughout. 4¾x6¼, saddlestitched, in Tweedweave wrappers. 250 numbered copies. Providence, 1973.

35. **Terry Stokes,** *Punching In, Punching Out* (poems). 24 pp. printed on recto. Handset in 12 pt. Caslon Oldstyle and printed letterpress

by Rosmarie Waldrop. 9½x6¼, saddlestitched, in Tweedweave wrappers. 250 numbered copies. Providence, 1973.

36. **Mark Strand,** *The Sargeantville Notebook* (poems). 24 pp. Handset in 12 pt. Caslon Oldstyle and printed letterpress on Warren Antique by Rosmarie Waldrop. 2 colors throughout. Cover by Keith Waldrop. 9½x6¼, saddlestitched, in Tweedweave wrappers. 400 numbered copies. Providence, 1973.

37. **John Taggart,** *Pyramid Canon* (poem sequence). 24 pp. printed on recto. Handset in 12 pt. Caslon Oldstyle and printed letterpress by Keith Waldrop. 3 colors throughout. 9½x6¼, saddlestitched, in Tweedweave wrappers. 250 numbered copies. Providence, 1973.

38. **George Tysh,** *Shop/Posh* (2 prose poems). 12 pp. printed on recto. Handset in 18 pt. Caslon Oldstyle and printed letterpress on Curtis Rag by Keith Waldrop. 2 colors throughout. 10x6, saddlestitched, in Tweedweave wrappers. 300 numbered copies. Providence, 1973.

39. **Keith & Rosmarie Waldrop,** *Until Volume One* (poems in collaboration). 34 pp. Handset in 12 pt. Caslon Oldstyle and printed letterpress on Warren Antique by Rosmarie Waldrop. 2 colors throughout. Cover by Keith Waldrop. 4¾x6¼, saddlestitched, in Tweedweave wrappers. 500 numbered copies. Providence, 1973.

40. **Keith & Rosmarie Waldrop,** *Words Worth Less* (7 transformations of "Tintern Abbey"). 24 pp. printed on recto. Handset in 12 pt. Caslon Oldstyle and printed letterpress on Warren Antique by Rosmarie Waldrop. 2 colors throughout. 9½x6¼, saddlestitched, in Tweedweave wrappers. 500 numbered copies. Providence, 1973.

41. **Tom Ahern,** *The Strangulation of Dreams* (a story). 16 pp. Offset. Cover printed letterpress by Keith Waldrop. 8½x6¼, saddlestitched. 250 copies. Providence, 1974.

42. **Anthony Barnett,** *Poem About Music.* 64 pp. Handset in 12 pt. Caslon Oldstyle and printed letterpress on Warren Antique by Rosmarie Waldrop. The offset cover reproduces a painting by Antonio Sena. 9x6, perfect-bound paperback. 950 copies. Providence, 1974.

42a. Same. Smythe-sewn clothback. 50 numbered, signed copies.

43. **Nancy Condee,** *The Rape of St. Emad* (prose poem). 16 pp. Handset in 18 pt. Caslon Oldstyle with 24 pt. Boulevard Caps and printed letterpress on Linweave Text by Keith Waldrop. The 2-color titlepage and cover have a drawing by Sophie Hawkes. 5x7, saddlestitched, in Cortlea wrappers. 300 numbered copies. Providence, 1974.

44. **Andrew Crozier,** *The Veil Poem* (10 poems and a coda). 28 pp. printed on recto. Handset in 12 pt. Caslon Oldstyle and printed letterpress on Warren Antique by George Hodgkins. 9½x6¼, saddlestitched, in Tweedweave wrappers. 300 numbered copies. Providence, 1974.

45. Ray DiPalma, *Max, a Sequel* (poems). 24 pp. Handset in 12 pt. Caslon Oldstyle and printed letterpress on Warren Antique by Rosmarie Waldrop. 9½x6¼, saddlestitched, in Tweedweave wrappers. 300 numbered copies. Providence, 1974.

46. Patrick Fetherston, *His Many and Himself* (poem). 28 pp. Handset in 12 pt. Caslon Oldstyle and printed letterpress on Warren Antique by Rosmarie Waldrop. 2 colors throughout. 9½x6¼, saddlestitched, in Cortlea wrappers. 350 numbered copies. Providence, 1974.

47. **George Hodgkins,** *Accidental Postures* (poems). 20 pp. printed on recto. Handset in 12 pt. Caslon Oldstyle and printed letterpress on Warren Antique by the author. 9½x6¼, saddlestitched, in Tweedweave wrappers. 350 numbered copies. Providence, 1974.

48. **Edwin Honig,** *At Sixes* (poems). 36pp. Handset in 12 pt. Caslon Oldstyle and printed letterpress on Warren Antique by George Hodgkins. 2 colors. 4¾x6¼, saddlestitched, in Tweedweave wrappers. 350 numbered copies. Providence, 1974.

49. **Jackson MacLow,** *4 Trains* (poems). 28 pp. Handset in 12 pt. Caslon Oldstyle & 30 pt. Bauer Topic and printed letterpress on Warren Antique by Rosmarie Waldrop. 2 colors. 9½x6¼, saddlestitched, in Tweedweave wrappers. 300 numbered copies. Providence, 1974.

50. **Harry Mathews,** *The Planisphere* (poems). 24 pp. Handset in 12 pt. Caslon Oldstyle and printed letterpress on Warren Antique by Rosmarie Waldrop. Cover by Keith Waldrop. 9½x6¼, saddlestitched, in Tweedweave wrappers. 350 numbered copies. Providence, 1974.

51. **Ron Silliman,** *nox* (poems). 34 pp. printed on recto. Handset in 12 pt. Caslon Oldstyle and printed letterpress on Curtis Rag by Rosmarie Waldrop. 2 colors throughout. 8½?7, saddlestitched, in Tweedweave wrappers. 300 numbered copies. Providence, 1974.

52. **Keith Waldrop,** *Fulfillment* (story). 26 pp. printed on recto. Offset. Cover and titlepage by the author. 8½x6¼, saddlestitched. 250 copies. Providence, 1974.

53. **Tom Ahern,** *The Sinister Pinafore* (poems). 16 pp. printed on recto. Handset in 12 pt. Caslon Oldstyle and printed letterpress on Warren Antique by Ardis Eichhorn. 9½x6¼, saddlestitched, in Cortlea wrappers. 300 numbered copies, signed on the cover. Providence, 1975.

54. **James Camp,** *Carnal Refreshment* (poems). 73 pp. Linotyped in 12 pt. Baskerville. Designed and printed letterpress on Warren Antique by Rosmarie Waldrop. Offset cover by Keith Waldrop. 9x6, perfect-bound paperback. 950 copies. Providence, 1975.

54a. Same. Smythe-sewn clothback. 50 numbered & signed copies.

55. **Ippy Gizzi,** *Letters to Pauline* (a sequence of prose poems with 15 drawings by the author). 40 pp. Offset from typewriter and ballpoint. Letterpress titlepage and cover by Keith Waldrop. 8½x7, saddlestitched. 300 copies. Providence, 1975.

56. **Charles Hine,** *Wild Indians* (poem). 38 pp. Handset in 12 pt. Caslon Oldstyle & 30 pt. Bauer Topic and printed letterpress on Warren Antique by Rosmarie Waldrop. Cover drawing by the author. 9½x6¼, saddlestitched, in Tweedweave wrappers. 340 numbered copies. Providence, 1975.

57. **Stephen Sandy,** *The Difficulty* (poem). 16 pp. Handset in 18 pt. Caslon Oldstyle and printed letterpress on Warren Antique by Joel Rosen. 2 colors throughout. 9½x6¼, saddlestitched, in Tweedweave wrappers. 300 numbered copies. Providence, 1975.

58. **Barton Levi St. Armand,** *Hypogeum* (poems of the buried life). 30 pp. Handset in 12 pt. Caslon Oldstyle and printed letterpress on Warren Antique by Keith Waldrop. 9½x6¼, saddlestitched, in Tweedweave wrappers. 350 numbered copies. Providence, 1975.

59. **Keith Waldrop,** *The Garden of Effort* (poems). 89 pp. Handset in 12 pt. Caslon Oldstyle & 18 pt. Berthold Post Roman and printed letterpress on Warren Antique by Rosmarie Waldrop. Cover by Keith Waldrop. 9x6, perfect-bound paperback. 950 copies. Providence, 1975.

59a. Same. Smythe-sewn clothback. 50 numbered & signed copies.

60. **Keith & Rosmarie Waldrop,** *Since Volume One* (poems in collaboration). 34 pp. Handset in 12 pt. Caslon Oldstyle and printed letterpress on Warren Antique by Rosmarie Waldrop. 2 colors throughout. Cover by Keith Waldrop. 4¾x6¼, saddlestitched. 500 numbered copies. Providence, 1975.

61. **David Ball,** *The Garbage Poems* (poem sequence). 28 pp. Text linotyped in 12 pt. Bodoni. Designed and printed letterpress on Warren Antique by Rosmarie Waldrop. 2 colors throughout. 9½x6¼, saddlestitched, in Strathmore Grandee wrappers. 350 numbered copies. Providence, 1976.

62. **Michael Gizzi,** *Bird As* (a poem in 8 parts). 20 pp. Handset in 12 pt. Caslon Oldstyle and printed letterpress on Warren Antique by Joel Rosen, Windfall Press. 2 colors throughout. 9½x6¼, saddlestitched, in Tweedweave wrappers printed both offset and letterpress. 350 numbered copies. Providence, 1976.

63. **Barbara Guest,** *The Countess from Minneapolis* (sequence of poems in prose and verse). 46 pp. Linotyped in 12 pt. Caledonia. Designed and printed letterpress on Warren Antique by Rosmarie Waldrop, with a 2-color title page. The offset cover by Keith Waldrop uses a reproduction of Robert Koehler's painting "Rainy Evening on Hennepin Avenue." 9x6, perfectbound paperback. 950 copies. Providence, 1976.

63 a. Same. Smythe-sewn clothback. 50 numbered & signed copies.

64. **Lissa McLaughlin,** *Approached by Fur* (prose poems). 28 pp. Handset in 12 & 24 pt. Caslon Oldstyle with 24 pt. Boulevard Caps and printed letterpress on Warren Antique by Keith Waldrop. 2 colors throughout. Cover drawing by the author. 9½x6¼, saddlestitched, in Strathmore Grandee wrappers, 324 numbered copies. Providence, 1976.

64a. Same. Printed on Rives Heavyweight, sewn, in Arches wrappers. 26 lettered & signed copies, each with an original drawing by the author.

65. **Debra Bruce,** *Dissolves* (poems). 16 pp. Handset in 12 pt. Caslon Oldstyle and printed letterpress on Warren Antique by Leigh Dingerson, with a 2-color title page. 9½x6¼, saddlestitched, in Strathmore Grandee wrappers. 350 numbered copies. Providence, 1977.

65a Same. Printed on Barcham Green Charter Oak, sewn, in Fabriano wrappers. 26 lettered & signed copies.

66. **David Chaloner,** *Projections* (poems). 24 pp. printed on recto. Handset in 12 pt. Caslon Oldstyle and printed letterpress on Warren

Antique by Rosmarie Waldrop, with a 2-color title page. 9½x6¼, saddlestitched, in Strathmore Grandee wrappers. 350 numbered copies. Providence, 1977.

67. Lyn Hejinian, *A Mask of Motion* (poems). 28 pp. Text linotyped in 12 pt. Caledonia. Designed and printed letterpress on Warren Antique by Rosmarie Waldrop. Title page in 2 colors. The cover drawing is by Eli M. Mile. 9½x6¼, saddlestitched, in Strathmore Americana wrappers. 350 numbered copies. Providence, 1977.

67a. Same. Printed on Rives Heavyweight, sewn, in Charter Oak wrappers. 26 lettered & signed copies.

68. Harry Mathews, *Trial Impressions* (30 variations on a song by John Dowland). 46 pp. Text linotyped in 12 pt. Baskerville. Designed and printed letterpress on Warren Antique by Rosmarie Waldrop, with the title page in 2 colors. Offset cover by Keith Waldrop. 9x6, perfectbound paperback, 950 copies. Providence, 1977.

68a. Same. Smythe-sewn clothback. 50 numbered & signed copies.

69. W. D. Snodgrass, *6 Troubadour Songs* (adaptations with music). 40 pp. Handset in 12 pt. Caslon Oldstyle and printed letterpress on Warren Antique by Rosmarie Waldrop. Melodies printed with the help of Andrew Sabol. Cover & design by Keith Waldrop. 9½x6¼, saddlestitched, in Strathmore Grandee wrappers. 500 copies. Providence, 1977.

69a. Same. Printed on Barcham Green Charter Oak, sewn, in Fabriano wrappers. 26 lettered & signed copies.

70. Marcia Southwick, *What the Trees Go Into* (poem in 5 parts). 16 pp. Handset in 12 pt. Caslon Oldstyle and printed letterpress on Warren Antique by Leigh Dingerson, with a title page in 2 colors. 9½x6¼, saddlestitched, in Strathmore Chroma wrappers. 350 numbered copies plus 26 lettered & signed. Providence, 1977.

71. Tom Ahern, *The Capture of Trieste* (8 stories). 66 pp. Designed and set in Bodoni Book by Joel Rosen. Offset. The cover reproduces a collage by Joel Rosen. 7¼x5, perfect-bound paperback. 950 copies. Published in association with Windfall Press, Cambridge, MA and Providence, 1978.

71a. Same. Smythe-sewn clothback. 50 numbered & signed copies.

72. Bruce Andrews, *Film Noir* (concrete poems). 24 pp. printed on recto. Handset in Caslon Oldstyle & Bank Gothic Medium and printed letterpress on Warren Antique by Rosmarie Waldrop. The offset cover reproduces a drawing by the author. 9½x6, saddlestitched. 324 numbered copies plus 26 lettered & signed. Providence, 1978.

73. William Bronk, *That Beauty Still* (4 poems). 12 pp. printed on recto. Handset in 18 pt. Caslon & wood initials and printed letterpress on Strathmore Pastell by Rosmarie Waldrop. 2 colors throughout. There are 3 different covers, each an original silk screen by Linda Lutes. 6⅜x9¼, saddlestitched. 500 numbered copies. Providence, 1978.

73a. Same. Printed on Barcham Green Charter Oak, sewn. 26 lettered & signed copies.

74. Phil Demise, *What I Don't Know For Sure* (poem in 31 parts). 38 pp. Handset in 18 pt. Caslon Oldstyle and printed letterpress on

Warren Antique by Rosmarie Waldrop. 2 colors throughout 4¾x6¼, saddlestitched, in Tweedweave wrappers. 324 numbered copies plus 26 lettered & signed. Providence, 1978.

75. **Walter Hall,** *Miners Getting Off the Graveyard* (poems). 70 pp. Text linotyped in 12 pt. Garamond. Designed and printed letterpress on Warren Olde Style by Rosmarie Waldrop, with the title page in 2 colors. Offset cover by Keith Waldrop. 9x6, perfect-bound paperback. 950 copies. Providence, 1978.

75a. Same. Smythe-sewn clothback. 50 numbered & signed copies.

76. **Ruth Krauss,** *When I Walk I Change the Earth* (poem). 16 pp. Handset in 12 pt. Caslon Oldstyle & 48 pt. Quill Script and printed letterpress on Warren Olde Style by Leigh Dingerson. 2 colors. Cover by Keith Waldrop. 9½x6¼, saddlestitched, in Strathmore Grandee wrappers. 500 numbered copies. Providence, 1978.

76a. Same. Printed on Barcham Green Charter Oak, sewn, in Fabriano wrappers. 26 lettered & signed copies.

77. **Christopher Middleton,** *Anasphere: le torse antique* (poem in 4 parts). 16 pp. Handset in 12 pt. Caslon Oldstyle and printed letterpress on Warren Antique by Rosmarie Waldrop. 2 colors throughout. Cover by Keith Waldrop. 9½x6¼, saddlestitched, in Strathmore Americana wrappers. 500 copies. Providence, 1979.

77a. Same. Printed on Barcham Green Charter Oak, sewn, in Fabriano wrappers. 26 lettered & signed copies.

78. **Larry Eigner,** *lined up bulk senses* (7 poems). 20 pp. printed on recto. Handset in 12 pt. Caslon Oldstyle and printed letterpress on Warren Olde Style by Keith Waldrop. 9½x4¼, saddlestitched, in Strathmore Americana wrappers. 500 copies. Providence, 1979.

79. **Kenward Elmslie,** *Communications Equipment* (poems). 16 pp. Text linotyped in 11 pt. Devinne. Designed and printed letterpress on Warren Olde Style by Rosmarie Waldrop. 2 colors throughout. 9½x6¼, saddlestitched, in Cortlea wrappers. 500 copies. Providence, 1979.

79a. **Same.** Printed on Barcham Green Charter Oak, sewn, in Fabriano wrappers. 26 lettered & signed copies.

80. **Patrick Fetherston,** *The World Was a Bubble* (biography of Sir Francis Bacon, in verse with prose interruptions). 52 pp. Text linotyped in 11 pt. Devinne. Designed and printed letterpress on Warren Olde Style by Rosmarie Waldrop, with the title page in 2 colors. Offset cover by Keith Waldrop. 9x6, perfect-bound paperback. 950 copies. Providence, 1979.

80a. Same. Smythe-sewn clothback. 50 numbered & signed copies.

81. **Calvin Forbes,** *From the Book of Shine* (poems). 24 pp. Text linotyped in 11 pt. Times Roman. Designed and printed letterpress on Warren Olde Style by Rosmarie Waldrop, with the title page in 2 colors. 9½x6¼, saddlestitched, in Strathmore Text wrappers. 350 numbered copies plus 26 lettered & signed. Providence, 1979.

82. **Michael Gizzi,** *Avis or The Replete Birdman* (poems). 66 pp. Text linotyped in 11 pt. Devinne. Designed and printed on Warren Olde Style by Rosmarie Waldrop, with the title page in 2 colors. Offset cover by Keith Waldrop. 9x6, perfect-bound paperback. 950 copies. Providence, 1979.

82a. Same. Smythe-sewn clothback. 50 numbered & signed copies.

83. **Jaimy Gordon,** *Circumspections from an Equestrian Statue* (novella). 76 pp. Set in Deepdene and P.T. Barnum by Serif Composition. Offset. Frontispiece and 5 ornamental initials by Dennis Hlynski. Cover & design by Keith Waldrop. 7¼x5, perfectbound paperback. 950 copies. Providence, 1979.

83a. Same. Smythe-sewn clothback. 50 numbered & signed copies.

84. **Susan Hankla,** *I Am Running Home* (poems). 16 pp. Text lino-typed in 12 pt. Caledonia. Designed and printed letterpress on Warren Olde Style by Rosmarie Waldrop. 2 colors throughout. 9½x6¼, saddlestitched, in Strathmore Grandee wrappers. 324 numbered copies plus 26 lettered & signed. Providence, 1979.

85. **Lissa McLaughlin,** *Seeing the Multitudes Delayed* (14 stories). 76 pp. Set in 11 pt. Deepdene. Offset. Designed by Keith Waldrop. Cover drawing and 14 ornamental initials by the author. 7¼x5, perfect-bound paperback. 950 copies. Providence, 1979.

85a. Same. Smythe-sewn clothback. 50 numbered & signed copies.

86. **David Miller,** *Primavera* (a poem in 10 parts). 14 pp. Handset in 12 pt. Caslon Oldstyle and printed letterpress on Warren Olde Style by Ann Hohenstein. 2 colors throughout. 4¾x6¼, saddlestitched, in Strathmore Grandee wrappers. 324 numbered copies plus 26 lettered & signed. Providence, 1979.

87. **George Tysh,** *Tea* (poems). 22 pp. Text linotyped in 11 pt. Times Roman. Designed and printed letterpress on Warren Olde Style by Rosmarie Waldrop, with the title page in 2 colors. The offset cover reproduces a drawing by Jean-Louis Guy. 9¼x6¼, saddlestitched. 350 numbered copies plus 26 lettered & signed. Providence, 1979.

88. **Keith Waldrop,** *Egotistical Particulars.* 24 collages reproduced by color xerox and tipped onto Strathmore Pastell. 6¼x9¼, sewn into various wrappers. 100 copies. Providence, 1979.

89. **William Doreski,** *Half Of the Map* (a sequence of 22 poems). 24 pp. Text linotyped in 11 pt. Devinne. Designed and printed letter-press on Warren Olde Style by Pitt Harding. 2 colors throughout. 7x8, saddlestitched, in Classic Laid wrappers. 375 numbered copies plus 26 lettered & signed. Providence, 1980.

90. **Russell Edson,** *With Sincerest Regrets* (prose poems). 31 pp. Text linotyped in 11 pt. Devinne. Designed and printed letterpress on Warren Olde Style by Rosmarie Waldrop, with the title page in 2 colors. The cover drawing is by the author. 9½x6¼, saddlestitched, in Artemis wrappers. 500 copies. Providence, 1980.

90a. Same. Printed on Barcham Green Charter Oak, sewn, in Fabriano wrappers. 26 lettered & signed copies.

91. **John Engman,** *Alcatraz* (poems). 20 pp. Text linotyped in 11 pt. Devinne. Designed and printed letterpress on Warren Olde Style by Pitt Harding, with the title page in 2 colors. 9½x7, saddle-stitched, in Classic Laid wrappers. 350 numbered copies plus 26 lettered & signed. Providence, 1980.

92. **Harrison Fisher,** *The Text's Boyfriend* (poems). 18 pp. Text lino-typed in 11 pt. Devinne. Designed and printed letterpress on Warren Olde Style by Jennifer Montgomery, with the title page

in 2 colors. Cover by Keith Waldrop. 9½x6¼, saddlestitched, in Strathmore Brigadoon wrappers. 350 numbered copies plus 26 lettered & signed. Providence, 1980.

93. **Barbara Guest,** *Biography* (a poem in 9 parts). Text linotyped in 11 pt. Devinne. Designed and printed letterpress on Warren Olde Style by Rosmarie Waldrop. 2 colors throughout. Cover by Keith Waldrop. 9½x6¼, saddlestitched, in Classic Laid wrappers. 500 copies. Providence, 1980.

93a. Same. Printed on Barcham Green Charter Oak, sewn, in Fabriano wrappers. 26 lettered & signed copies.

94. **Lyn Hejinian,** *My Life* (short novel). 89 pp. Set in Devinne & Palatino. Offset. Design and cover by Keith Waldrop. 7¼x5, perfect-bound paperback. 950 copies. Providence, 1980.

94a. Same. Smythe-sewn clothback. 50 numbered & signed copies.

95. **Harry Mathews,** *Country Cooking and Other Stories.* 88 pp. Text linotyped in 12 pt. Palatino. Printed letterpress on Warren Olde Style by Rosmarie Waldrop, with the title page in 2 colors. Design, 7 ornamental initials and offset cover by Keith Waldrop. 7¼x5, perfect-bound paperback. 1400 copies. Providence, 1980.

95a. Same. Smythe-sewn clothback. 100 numbered & signed copies.

96. **Heather S. J. Steliga,** *Water Runs To What Is Wet* (poems). 55 pp. Text linotyped in 12 pt. Palatino. Designed and printed letterpress on Warren Olde Style by Rosmarie Waldrop, with the title page in 2 colors. Offset cover by Ibrahim Benoh. 9x6, perfect-bound paperback. 950 copies. Providence, 1980.

96a. Same. Smythe-sewn clothback, 50 numbered & signed copies.

97. **Rosmarie Waldrop,** *When They Have Senses* (sequence of poems). 82 pp. Text linotyped in 11 pt. Devinne. Designed and printed letterpress on Warren Olde Style by Rosmarie Waldrop, with the title page in 2 colors. The offset cover by Keith Waldrop reproduces a collage by Dorle Engelhardt. 9x6, perfect-bound paperback. 950 copies. Providence, 1980.

97a. Same. Smythe-sewn clothback. 50 numbered & signed copies.

98. **Tom Mandel,** *Erat* (3 long poems in prose and verse). 30 pp. Text linotyped in 12 pt. Palatino. Designed and printed letterpress on Warren Olde Style by Pitt Harding, with title page and 3 half titles in color. 9½x6¼, saddlestitched, in Strathmore Chroma wrappers. 450 numbered copies plus 26 lettered & signed. Providence, 1981.

99. **Stephen Wallin,** *Providence* (a sequence of poems). 20 pp. Text linotyped in 12 pt. Devinne. Designed and printed letterpress on Warren Olde Style by Jennifer Montgomery, with the title page in 2 colors. Cover by Keith Waldrop. 9½x6¼, saddlestitched, in Strathmore Text wrappers. 350 numbered copies plus 26 lettered & signed. Providence, 1981. ,

100. **John Yau,** *Broken Off By the Music* (3 poem sequences). 54 pp. Text linotyped in 12 pt. Devinne. Designed and printed letterpress on Warren Olde Style by Rosmarie Waldrop, with the title page and 3 half titles in 2 colors. Offset cover by Keith Waldrop. 9x6, perfect-bound paperback. 950 copies. Providence, 1981.

100a. Same. Smythe-sewn clothback. 50 numbered & signed copies.

"BURNING DECK BOOKS" PUBLISHED BY GEORGE WITTENBORN CO., New York:

1. **Keith Waldrop** and **Nelson Howe**, *To the Sincere Reader* (14 collages by Nelson Howe using a poem by Keith Waldrop). 28 pp. printed on recto. Printed letterpress from cuts by the author and artist at the Burning Deck press. 11½x8¾, saddlestitched. 3 colors throughout. 100 numbered and signed copies. New York, 1969.

2. **Rosmarie Waldrop** and **Nelson Howe**, *Body Image* (13 photo-collages by Nelson Howe using a poem by Rosmarie Waldrop). 17 sheets unbound in cloth folder. 2 color offset printing. 7¼x16½. 125 numbered & signed copies. New York, 1970.

3. **Nelson Howe** and **Steve Hesterman**, *Job Art* (computer printout of non-symmetrical possibilities of a 16-dot square). 11x15, 3½" thick, 16 copies. New York, 1971.

MAGAZINE:

James Camp, D.C. Hope, Bernard Waldrop (eds.), *Burning Deck* (a magazine of poetry and reviews of books "of interest to readers of poetry"). Handset and linotyped, printed letterpress. 8¾x5½.

#1. Poems by **Dallas Wiebe, Robert Creeley, Richard Emil Braun, Martin Lieberman, Theodore Holmes, Anne Stevenson, Edwin Honig, Robert Duncan, Dorothy Donnelly, Bert Meyers, Christopher Middleton, Louis Zukofsky.** Cover by Keith Waldrop. 1500 copies. Ann Arbor, MI, 1962.

#2. Poems by **Barbara Moraff, John Heath-Stubbs, Donald Finkel, Patricia Hooper, Robert Duncan, Rosmarie Keith, LeRoi Jones, Richard Gilbertson, Denise Levertov, Robert Clayton Casto, John L'Heureux.** Cover linoleum cut by Linda Lutes. 1000 copies. Ann Arbor, MI, 1963.

#3. Poems by **Laurel Johnson, Bernard Stempek, Robert Creeley, Kathleen Fraser, Barbara Guest, Harriet Stolorow, Gwyn Williams, Constance Urdang, Doris Parsons, Raeburn Miller, Valerie Worth, Natalie S. Robins, Glauco Cambon,** and a story by **Fielding Dawson.** Cover by Mary Ashley. 1000 copies. Ann Arbor, MI, 1963.

#4. Poems by **Peyton Houston, X.J. Kennedy, Clayton Eshleman, Dorothy Dalton, W.D. Snodgrass, Philip Levine, Christopher Middleton, W.S. Merwin, Carl Morse, Walter Hall, Robert Kelly, Theodore Enslin.** Cover by Nelson Howe. 700 copies. Durham, CT, 1965.

BROADSIDES:

1. **Diane Wakoski**, "Sometimes a Poet Will Hijack the Moon." Handset in Caslon Oldstyle and printed letterpress on Linweave Text by Keith Waldrop. 4 colors. 10x11. 300 copies. Providence, 1972.

2. **William Bronk**, "The Fragile Endurance of the World." Handset in Caslon Oldstyle with 24 pt. Boulevard Caps and printed letterpress on Tweedweave Cover by Keith Waldrop. 3 colors. 20x14. 100 copies. Providence, 1974.

3. Linda Lutes, 7 *Poets* 7 *Poems* (7 broadsides, each containing a silk screen portrait of the poet with a poem: **Michael Benedikt, William Bronk, Michael Harper, Edwin Honig, Rochelle Owens, Diane Wakoski, Rosmarie Waldrop**). Silk screened by the artist on Cranes Art Parchment. 15x20, folded once, in portfolio signed by the artist. 75 copies. Providence, 1974.

3a. Single broadsides, 16x20, unfolded, signed by artist and poet. 200 copies.

4. **Diane Wakoski,** "Love, the Lizard." Handset in Caslon Oldstyle and Cheltenham and printed letterpress on Tweedweave by Rosmarie Waldrop. 3 colors. 13x10. 300 copies. Providence, 1975.

POSTCARDS:

Handset in various typefaces and printed letterpress on a variety of cover stock by Keith and Rosmarie Waldrop, collected in 7x10 envelopes in sets of ten.

A. *Poem Postcards: The First Ten.* 100 envelopes. Providence, 1974.
   1. William Bronk, "The Fragile Endurance of the World". 1974.
   2. James Camp. "Out of the Crock." 1972.
   3. Tom Disch, "The William Tell Overture." 1972.
   4. George Hodgkins, "There Is No Need to Listen." 1973.
   5. -Eli M. Mile, "What Are You Going to Write?" 1972.
   6. Diane Wakoski, "A Lover Disregards Names." 1973.
   7. Keith Waldrop, "Enormouse." 1972.
   8. Rosmarie Waldrop, "The Word Is In." 1972.
   9. Brick Washington, "Catechumen's Appointment." 1972.
   10. Kirk Wilson, "God." 1972.

B. *Poem Postcards: The Second Ten.* 100 envelopes. Providence, 1974.
   11. James Camp, "The Gnostic World View." 1974.
   12. Nancy Condee, "Three Women." 1973.
   13. Tom Disch, "The Constellations." 1974.
   14. Ray Ragosta, "The Dancer." 1974.
   15. Carl Sesar, "Experience of Eternity." 1974.
   16. Mark Strand, "The Wisdom of a Dull Man." 1974.
   17. John Taggart, "Stone." 1974.
   18. Diane Wakoski, "Claws." 1973.
   19. Keith Waldrop, "Texture." 1974.
   20. Kirk Wilson, "Texas." 1973.

C. *Poem Postcards: The Third Ten.* 150 envelopes. Providence, 1975.
   21. Aliki Barnstone, "Why I Don't Write Poems."
   22. Michael Benedikt, "A Bad First Impression."
   23. James Camp, "Plaidland Redemption Center."
   24. Nancy Condee, "Saint Agnes Goes to the Circus."
   25. E. Hope-McCarthy, "Clean."
   26. Lissa McLaughlin, "The Snake."
   27. Eli M. Mile, "We Were Talking."
   28. Arthur Oberg, "Loving."
   29. Diane Wakoski, "Comparison." 1972.
   30. Rosmarie Waldrop, "Looking for Your."

D. *Poem Postcards: The Fourth Ten.*150 envelopes. Providence, 1978.
   31. Tom Ahern, "Opening the Umbrella."
   32. Gordon Anderson, "Couplets."
   33. William Bronk, "In the Beauty of the World."
   34. Denice Joan Deitch, "Epic Telephone Booth."
   35. Larry Eigner, "Running Around."
   36. Curtis Faville, "Dot."
   37. Susan Goldwitz, "Kali's Appetite."
   38. Ruth Krauss, "I Love You with the Aid of Brecht."
   39. Keith Waldrop, "Triple City."
   40. Rosmarie Waldrop, "Give Back What Disappears."
E. Uncollected:
   41. Rick Patrick, "Up Against the Wall." 1970.
   42. Alan Sondheim, "Snow." 1970.
   43. Keith Waldrop, "Dejection, an Ode." 1970.
   44. Stephanie Hine, "2 Towns in New England." 1972.

MISCELLANEOUS PUBLICATIONS:

1. **Keith Waldrop,** *Keith Tank Line* (poems). 7 sheets unbound in an envelope. Handset in 12 pt. Caslon Oldstyle and printed letterpress by the author. 9x6. 95 numbered envelopes. Durham, CT, 1966.

2. **Keith Waldrop,** *Poem in Return for a Present.* 20 pp. printed on recto. Handset in 18 pt. Caslon Oldstyle and printed letterpress on Tweedweave by Rosmarie Waldrop. Cover by Keith Waldrop. 4x11, saddle-stitched. 10 numbered & signed copies. Providence, 1969.

3. **Christopher Montgomery,** *Connecticut Elegy* (a record). Songs for voice and guitar with texts by James Camp, X. J. Kennedy, Keith Waldrop. Monaural. 500 copies. Providence, 1969.

4. **Christopher Montgomery,** *"Connecticut Elegy"* (sheet music). 1 sheet, 11x8½, folded. Offset. Text by Keith Waldrop. 100 copies. Providence, 1699.

5. *Transubstantiations of the John Barton Wolgamot Society,* I: 1. Hannah Arendt, "Reflections on Violins." 4 pp. Mimeographed. 14x8½, stapled. 100 copies. Bedford, MA & Providence, 1969.

6. *Transubstantiations of the John Barton Wolgamot Society,* II. 1. Tom Ahern, "Rat Song." 9 pp. Mimeographed. 14x8½, stapled. 100 copies. Bedford, MA & Providence, 1970.

7. *Transubstantiations of the John Barton Wolgamot Society,* II: 3. Transubstantiations of Meynell, Byron, Wordsworth. Ruth Montgomery on the non-existence of James Camp. 6 pp. Mimeographed. 14x8½, stapled. 100 copies. Bedford, MA, 1971.

8. **Carol LaBranche,** *A Small Joining* (concrete poems). 8 sheets loose in an envelope. Offset from handwriting. Hand coloring and collage by the author. 11x8½. 250 copies, Providence, 1971.

9. **Michael Harper,** "Lathe: Shirl's Tree" (poem and birth announcement for Rachel Maria). Broadside. Handset in Caslon Oldstyle and printed letterpress on Curtis Rag by Keith Waldrop. 8½x14, fo'ded once. 100 copies. Providence, 1972.

10. **Keith & Rosmarie Waldrop,** *Alice ffoster-Fallis* (an outline). "Wolgamotica, series Pseudomena," vol. 1. 22 pp. Offset from typewriter. 8½x7, saddlestitched. 100 copies. Providence, 1972.

11. **Eli M. Mile,** *An Intellectual Discussion.* "Wolgamotica, series Pseudomena," vol. 2. 26 pp. Offset from typewriter. 8½x7, saddlestitched. 100 copies. Providence, 1972.

12. **Chisholm Quince,** *On Seeing Wordsworth's Sandwich Box at the Dove Cottage Museum, Grasmere, July 1, 1970* (poem). "Wolgamotica, series Immemorabilia," vol. 1. 1 sheet, 14x8½ folded once. Offset from handwriting. 100 copies. Providence, 1972.

13. **James Camp,** *Food Thoughts* (poem, with blergs by Jocelyn Camp). "Wolgamotica, series Spaghettica," vol. 1. 1 sheet, 14x8½, folded once. Offset from typewriter and ballpoint. 100 copies. Providence, 1973.

14. **Eli M. Mile,** 5 *Potholders* (poems). "Wolgamotica, series Spaghettica," vol. 2. 6 pp. Offset from typewriter. 8½x7, saddlestitched. 100 copies. Providence, 1973.

15. **Eli M. Mile,** *She Runs a Tight Ship* (an intellectual discussion). "Wolgamotica, series Pseudomena," vol. 3. 12 pp. Offset from typewriter. 8½x7, saddlestitched. 100 copies. Providence, 1973.

16. **Carl Morse,** *Turtle Flow* (poems). "Wolgamotica, series Macaronica," vol. 1. 12 pp. Offset from typewriter. 8½x7, saddlestitched. 100 copies. Providence, 1973.

17. **Ruth Rosenbaum,** *Paradox Lost, or, The Forbidden Fortune Cookie* (play). "Wolgamotica, series Puntheistica," vol. 1. 12 pp. Offset from typewriter. 8½x7, saddlestitched. 100 copies. Providence, 1973.

18. **Keith Waldrop,** (translator), *Stephane Mallarme: The Demon of Analogy.* 1 sheet, 14x8½ folded once. Offset from handwriting. 25 copies. Providence, 1974.

19. **Keith Waldrop,** *An Unfortunate Experience with the Offset Press.* 1 sheet, 14x8½, folded once and crumpled. Offset. 25 copies. Providence, 1974.

The text of this book was linotyped in 10 pt. Caledonia by Mollohan Typesetting in West Warwick, RI. Designed and printed by Rosmarie Waldrop, with an offset cover by Keith Waldrop. Smythe-sewn by New Hampshire Bindery. There are 1500 copies, of which 100 are cloth-bound.